The Development
of Writing
in Children

Pre-K Through Grade 8

The Development
of Writing
in Children

Pre-K Through Grade 8

Marvin L. Klein
Western Washington University

PRENTICE-HALL, INC.   Englewood Cliffs, New Jersey 07632

Library of Congress Cataloging in Publication Data

Klein, Marvin L.
  The development of writing in children.

  Bibliography: p.
  Includes index.
  1. Children—Writing.   I. Title.
  LB1139.W7K57   1985   372.6′23   83-26846
  ISBN 0-13-208141-5

Editorial/production supervision and
  interior design: Sylvia Schmokel and Sylvia Moore
Cover design: George Cornell
Manufacturing buyer: Ron Chapman

L B
1139
,W7
K57
1985

Printed in the United States of America

10   9   8   7   6   5   4   3   2   1

ISBN 0-13-208141-5 01

Prentice-Hall International, Inc., *London*
Prentice-Hall of Australia Pty. Limited, *Sydney*
Editora Prentice-Hall do Brasil, Ltda., *Rio de Janeiro*
Prentice-Hall Canada Inc., *Toronto*
Prentice-Hall of India Private Limited, *New Delhi*
Prentice-Hall of Japan, Inc., *Tokyo*
Prentice-Hall of Southeast Asia Pte. Ltd., *Singapore*
Whitehall Books Limited, *Wellington, New Zealand*

Contents

3

Helping the Preschool/Kindergarten Child Develop Writing Abilities

4

Writing Development through the Elementary and Middle School Years

5

Designing a Writing Curriculum for Grades 1 through 8

6

Writing Activities and Teaching Ideas for Grades 1 through 8   109

7

Evaluating Writing and Monitoring Writing Progress   162

The Development
of Writing
in Children
Pre-K Through Grade 8

Introduction

chapter

1

When *do* children learn to write? When *can* children learn to write? And, how can we assist children in learning to write? These are three major questions that govern the content of this book. However, before we can address even the first of these, a fundamental question central to all three must be considered, namely, What is writing?

Melissa is in kindergarten. Figure 1–1 shows a sample of her "writing."

Figure 1–1.

When Erika, Melissa's older sister, was in the first grade, she produced the "writing" in Figure 1–2.

Rhonda, a second-grader, shared the story shown in Figure 1–3 with her teacher and friends.

Dawn is a 4-year-old not yet in school but prolific with paper and pencil. She recently composed a story for her father (see Figure 1–4). It is about three bears lost in a forest.

And, one last example for consideration here. Brina, a 5-year-old Russian child given a series of sentences to remember, recorded "A man has two arms and two legs" with the following marks:

She then read the sentence using the marks she made on the paper as cues.

Which of these children knows how to write? If one defines "*writing*" in a manner that excludes all but cursively produced expression, then only Rhonda knows how to write. If one means by "writing" the ability to use necessary

Figure 1–2.

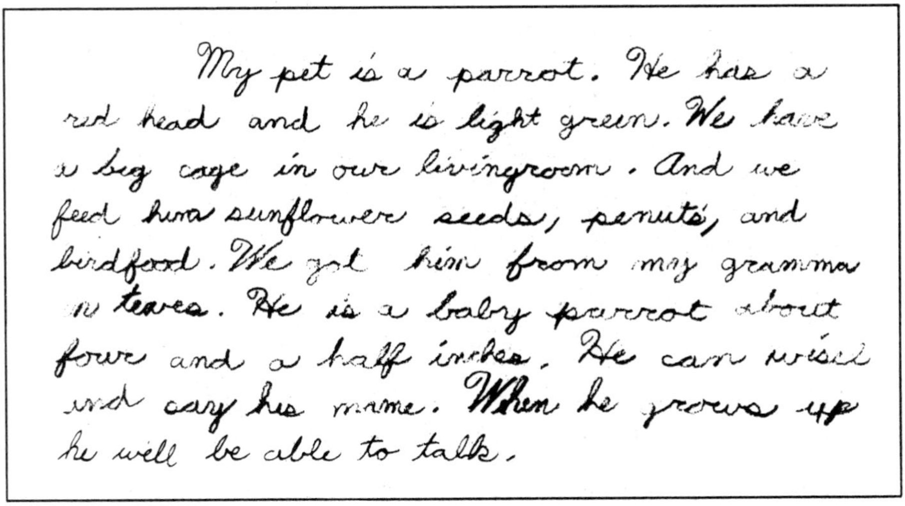

My pet is a parrot. He has a
red head and he is light green. We have
a big cage in our livingroom. And we
feed him sunflower seeds, penuts, and
birdfood. We got him from my gramma
n teaves. He is a baby parrot about
four and a half inches. He can wisil
nd say his name. When he grows up
he will be able to talk.

Figure 1–3.

Figure 1–4.

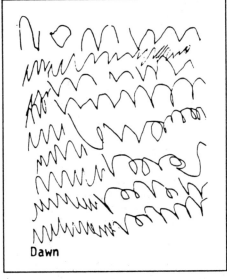

Dawn

instruments of composition to produce letters of the alphabet in either manuscript (block printing) or cursive style to form words and sentences, then Rhonda is still our only writer. If, by "writing," we mean the ability to form letters of the alphabet on paper regardless of their communication role, then our kindergartener, Melissa, is also a writer.

And finally, if we mean by "writing," *"the ability to employ pen or pencil and paper to express ideas symbolically so that the representations on the paper reflect meaning and content capable of being communicated to another by the producer using the marks as mnemonic cues,''* then *all* of the preceding examples are writing.

It is this last definition of writing that provides the basis for our approach to this critical area of language use by young children. This is not to suggest that the other definitions are not important or useful, since they obviously are. However, by making some definitional distinctions, we are more likely to understand the limits as well as the potential of our concerns about the development of writing in young children.

"Handwriting" is often used synonymously with "writing" by many. Commercial handwriting programs normally include steps and procedures for producing written language in both manuscript and cursive form in their materials. In this book we, too, shall talk about "handwriting," but our concerns include composition and the associated requisite skills and knowledge. In some senses, it would be possible for a child to learn how to "handwrite" in the sense of form/block print letters—as many kindergarteners can—and yet be unable to write! Learning how to form letters can be simply a mechanical act divorced from any intent to communicate information to another—indeed, contemporary research suggests that this often happens in the early school years. On the other hand, it is quite possible for a young child to understand the functions and general features of writing before he or she has mastered letter-forming skills.

To be an effective writer, one must fully understand and master the expressive skills implicit in the ideas of "writing-as-mechanical-act" and "writing-as-conceptual-act." Learning to go through the mechanics of producing letters and words on paper must be accompanied by a developing perception of writing as an expressive skill for communicating information, as an abstracting and symbolizing tool capable of shaping as well as sharing ideas.

In order to allow for the incorporation of both of these notions within the general concerns of educators, some researchers and theoreticians prefer to use the term *written expression* to describe the early writing efforts of children before they have acquired the necessary letter-producing skills. This, however, is a subtle distinction and can lead to confusion in identifying a given child's abilities in the early years. So-called scribble writing, for example, may be produced by a child who yet has no grasp of writing as a conceptual tool. Many children, especially between the ages of 3 and 5, often engage in activities described as scribble writing when they are merely imitating the actions of adults. They may very well have a sense of this activity as something valued in society and something done by people which is important in their lives; therefore, by association, these expressive actions bear imitating. However, they do not bear symbolic or communicative potential.

Other children, incapable of or not yet taught the skills of letter and word formation, still have an understanding of writing's symbolizing and communication potential. They apparently are aware that the marks on the paper serve important communication and symbolizing roles. In short, some scribble writers are relatively advanced achievers of written expression, while others are simply imitators at this point in their development.

With older children there often remains an inability to distinguish between writing-as-mechanical-act and writing-as-conceptual-act. Educators often try to distinguish between the two by referring to the former as "scripting," or simply recording information such as grocery lists or simple direction giving, and "composing," putting ideas into written form.

With these definitions in mind then let us consider several important points:

1. "Writing" refers to the ability to use pen and paper to denote ideas or facts in a symbolic fashion. This implies also the ability to use those marks as mnemonic cues (to aid memory) or idea cues.
2. "Written expression" refers to the pen/paper productions of the younger child that have symbolic value but are not necessarily presented in the standard and commonly accepted mode of alphabetic letters (in either the print or cursive form).
3. *Handwriting* is a term used to describe the expression of letters and words in *either* print or cursive form.
4. Written expression is a form of writing, albeit one normally perceived as appearing in the earlier period of the developing writer.
5. A young child is capable of writing and often produces writing *prior* to the possession of handwriting skills. However, many authorities prefer to refer to such production as "written expression" rather than as "writing."
6. Some scribble writing is written expression; some is not. It depends upon whether the producer intends the result to reflect idea communication where the ideas are assumed to be characterized by the marks functioning as symbols on the paper.
7. Some types of drawings or pictures may be employed as written expression. When they are used this way, rather than as art per se, they are referred to as *pictographs.*
8. It is quite possible for a child to possess handwriting skills and employ them in varying settings *without* having the ability to write.
9. Writing-as-mechanical-act and writing-as-conceptual-act develop through the elementary school years but are often not perceived as separate notions by teacher or child.

These points serve critical roles in our assumptions about writing development in the preschool and early school years.

Understanding these ideas does not help us in considering a more fundamental question that may be central to any consideration of writing and its development in children, namely, Why is writing important? Is writing as critical as most educators contend? With advances in computer age technology and various electronic communication modes, do children need to develop writing abilities?

It is important to consider that writing serves several different general functions in our lives. One use of writing is to communicate with another, information transmission. This is the most commonly assumed purpose and, in the minds of many, the only functional purpose of writing. However, it is this function that is most susceptible to the assertions of the electronic age communications advocates who suggest that writing as a personal act is outdated.

We should note, though, a second function of writing. Writing is an important means of self-expression. It has therapeutic value and serves as an important emotions expression outlet. Further, its aesthetic potential is well known. A poet seldom writes a poem simply to communicate with another. There are more fundamental personal reasons motivating the act. A language philosopher once observed that "language is the house in which we live." Writing, as a critical manifestation of our language, is a major vehicle for self-discovery and self-expression not possible in any other symbolic mode. In short, we would "write" even if there were no need to communicate information to another; personal need would dictate that we do so.

There is also a third, and possibly more important, reason for writing. Writing assists the development of thinking and learning generally. James Britton, a British authority in this area, asserts, "We learn by writing, and we learn to write by writing." And the order of these two points is of some significance. Whether or not an idea becomes more explicit in the written product may be less relevant to the child than is the process of attempting the writing itself.[1] W. Stern asserts that recognition of the fact that linguistic signs have meaning constitutes the greatest discovery in the child's life.[2] Lev Vygotsky, a noted Russian developmental psychologist, has observed, "The most significant moment in the course of intellectual development, which gives birth to the purely human forms of practical and abstract intelligence, occurs when speech and practical activity, two previously completely independent lines of development, converge."[3] Later, in the same work, Vygotsky points to both play and writing as important aspects of the individual's developing perception of language as a symbolizing tool and as an important link in the development of higher psychological processes. And certainly writing constitutes one of the more demanding forms of symbol/mind interplay. It implicitly requires the individual to draw upon a second-order level of abstraction (speaking or oral language being a first-order level of abstraction) for translating cognitive operations into observable product, even though the product is not likely to be equal to the potential of the interplay of mind and sign. We can always know more than we can tell.[4]

In short, we wish to assert the following:

1. Initially, in the life of the child, thought is not language-dependent.
2. With the onset of oral language, the child possesses an expressive mode for nonverbal thought.
3. The convergence of thought and language, where the two interplay to reinforce the growth and potential of each other, is a critical development in the child.
4. The evolution of an increasingly sophisticated perception of symbol and its potential for enhancing and exploiting one's cognitive facilities occurs through the development and use of play and written expression in the child.

Justification for writing as a worthwhile educational enterprise transcends notions that reduce it to its more mundane roles. Writing is critical for many reasons, not the least of which is in helping the writer become a more effective thinker and learner.

What follows in this book will draw heavily from the preceding and will derive from certain basic assumptions. These are:

1. The development of writing is a critical element in the child's education.
2. Writing is fundamental to both the development of expressive facility with language and to more sophisticated intellectual growth.
3. Writing evolves naturally in the young child, and the characteristics of this evolution can provide an instructional framework for enhancing this natural development.
4. Writing development takes place over the spectrum of what is usually considered the early childhood and elementary school years, prekindergarten through grade 8, and beyond.
5. Both parents and educators can assist significantly in the development of writing in young children.
6. Writing instruction should constitute a significant portion of the entire elementary school curriculum.

NOTES

1. L. Vygotsky, *Mind in Society* (Cambridge: Harvard University Press, 1978); L. Vygotsky, *Thought and Language* (Cambridge: MIT Press, 1962); and H. Werner and B. Kaplan, *Symbol Formation* (New York: John Wiley, 1963).

2. W. Stern, *Psychology of Early Childhood Up to the Sixth Year of Age* (New York: Holt, Rinehart & Winston, 1924).

3. Vygotsky, *Mind in Society*, p. 24.

4. M. Klein, "Language and the Child: A Few Key Generalizations," *Educational Leadership* (March 1981): 446–48.

Writing Development in the Young Child, Ages 3 to 6

chapter

2

THE CHILD AS LINGUIST: ORAL LANGUAGE USER

A few years ago a popular reading program included in its opening materials for teachers the observation that an adult looking at a totally unfamiliar language—Greek, for example—was like a kindergarten or first-grade child looking at the print in the primer volumes of a basal reading program for the first time. What the child sees is simply an array of unusual squiggles or marks completely unrelated to the real world as he or she knows it.

Today there are few people who would still agree with this analogy. Ours is a print- and writing-dominated society, and from the very earliest years, children are bombarded with written and oral language in a variety of forms. Preschool children, for the most part, have a reasonable grasp of the functions of language, what it is and why it is employed.[1] And, although there obviously are exceptions, most children entering school are reasonably elegant producers and consumers of language in a variety of forms.

Four-year-old children, shown a box of Jello, for example, will commonly observe, "That says 'strawberry seeds,'" or "That says 'strawberry mix.'" Shown a Gleem toothpaste box, they read, "That says 'Brush your teeth every day'" or some such.[2] Perhaps they are not "decoding" the sound-letter correspondences that constitute the actual words presented. However, most of our general definitions of "reading" may be perceived in such a way that the above observations by the children involved were examples of their "reading." These children could utilize their personal experience, background, and knowledge of the important elements of society around them in deriving meaning from or imparting mean-ing to (depending upon your individual definition of the process) the messages presented.

During the past several years, in fact, we have learned that children from birth to beginning school age know a great deal about language generally, its functions and its uses. Researchers in language development (often referred to as develop-mental psycholinguists in the profession) point to a surprising range of language skills quite early on in the child. Lois Bloom, for example, notes the early apprecia-tion of the ''speech act'' as a shaper of the meaning of an utterance. She cites, for instance, ''Mommy sock'' by her own child. In some cases the utterance was used to assert a proposition about the actions of the mother—she was picking up the sock or placing it in a drawer. In other cases, the assertion had to do with the child's description of her own acts or behavior—''I'm putting the sock on'' or the like.[3] The child, then, very early appreciates that the act of the asserting defines the meaning of the utterance as much as, if not more than, does the meaning of the individual vocabulary items within.

It is quite generally accepted now that the most productive growth years in language acquisition and development are between ages 2 and 5.[4] During this period of time, for example, the child typically masters the basic sentence structures and even a number of the more elegant expanded grammar constructions. By age 3, the child understands and uses subject-predicate relationships in utterances and operates with the main grammatical categories such as noun and verb.[5] The child develops at the same time an understanding that language can be put to a number of different uses—to inform, to request, to persuade—and that there is some sort of relationship between meaning and language function and between context of the language use and the way the language is used.[6]

Young children have learned these many aspects of language and its em-ployment before they ever enter school. They do so apparently by functioning as a sort of researcher themselves. They form hypotheses about what will work with the language by trying various ideas out in the language-using environment around them. If something works, keep it and reuse it, but if it doesn't work (isn't accept-able to those with whom you wish to communicate), chuck it and try something else: Thus seems to go the system that young language learners employ.

Their oral language is acquired in an orderly set of stages, each with its own generalized governing principles. They do not learn language by simply imitating adults, although living in a rich language-using environment is critical. Nor do they acquire language in an accidental fashion. Instead, language develops systemat-ically, and it becomes more complex and utterances more elegant through the years. Each of these various stages of development from beginning of speech through the beginning school years reflects attributes common to all children in the stage. Many of these attributes are quite different from those of adult language. For example, overextension of the -ed ending to inappropriate verbs is common in the grammar of children through kindergarten and first grade. ''I falled down'' or ''I hurted my knee'' are normal language uses at this stage. ''Because'' is used as a coordinating conjunction rather than as a cause-effect term by children through second grade.[7] Through the primary years, animistic verbs are often used with inanimate nouns— "the sun *chases* the clouds" or "the boat *wants* to go on the lake."[8]

In other words, many of the uses of language by young children appear initially to be strange or even anomalous compared to adult language. Yet, examination reveals children's language to be systematic, consistent, and in tune with careful testing techniques they have developed to try out their individual language systems.

By the age of 5, children have the necessary oral language skills for expressing ideas and concepts that their intellectual development is yet unable to generate. Yet, it is estimated that children at beginning school age have a comprehension vocabulary two times or more greater than that which they use in their own oral communication.[9] And it is now commonly accepted that language comprehension normally exceeds language production by a considerable amount for several years into the elementary grades.[10]

In brief, when it comes to oral language, children through the normal preschool range (through five years or so) are reasonable masters of the language structure, sound system, meaning and meaning formation system, and the varieties of purposes to which language may be put. More importantly, children have become relatively sophisticated hypothesizers, testers, explorers of and with language. Not only do they possess a great deal of language knowledge and skill in its use, but in addition they have developed the critical strategies and processes necessary for developing new language knowledge and new, more sophisticated skills in its employment.

Perhaps the most interesting aspect of this rather incredible feat is that this language development normally takes place without formal instruction, although it takes place more effectively in rich language-using environments, in homes where language is both respected and enjoyed and where parents make a conscious effort to provide an encouraging and responsive setting for developing children.[11]

At first glance, this consideration of oral language development may seem to be tangential to writing development in children and thus outside the purview of this book. However, this is not the case. In fact, the oral language base is the primary language source the child has for developing a full range of language-producing and -consuming skills, including writing. It is the first language and the first-level abstraction of language. All other modes—listening, reading, and writing—are all second-level abstractions, language uses filtered through the first abstraction, oral language. Oral language ability determines in large measure facility with the other language modes. In short, this means that oral language facility is critical to the development of written expression.

Consider the importance of oral language. In reference to the intellectual development of the young child, Vygotsky asserts: "The history of the process of the internalization of social speech is also the history of the socialization of children's practical intellect."[12] Again, on the relationship of oral language to the development of perceptual abilities, Vygotsky notes: "Our research has shown that even at very early stages of development, language and perception are linked.''[13] In his research with preschoolers (ages 3 to 5) Vygotsky found that

> speech not only accompanies practical activity but also plays a specific role in carrying it out. Our experiments demonstrate two important facts:
> 1. A child's speech is as important as the role of action in attaining goals. Children not only speak about what they are doing, their speech and action are part of one and the same complex psychological function, directed toward the solution of the problem at hand.
> 2. The more complex the action demanded by the situation and the less direct its solution, the greater the importance played by speech in the operation as a whole. Sometimes speech becomes of such vital importance that, if not permitted to use it, young children cannot accomplish the given task.
> These observations lead me to the conclusion that children solve practical tasks with the help of their speech, as well as their eyes and hands.[14]

In a contemporary reinforcing note, Rupley and Russell, summarizing results of their research review of recent studies in language development, observed, ''Providing a climate that stimulates language activity and emphasizes language use should promote language development.''[15]

In addition to the large body of literature addressing language development generally in young children and how to facilitate its more positive fruition, there are a number of studies that address the attributes of language use for functional purpose and the extent to which such facility in the young language user correlates with the various features and structures of language normally associated with more linguistically capable or advanced children. Joan Tough, for example, explored such functional uses of language by children. She categorized discourse samples according to the appropriateness of form and purpose and according to syntactical (grammatical) complexity and semantic (meaning) richness. Her subjects were children from 3½ to 7 years of age.[16]

Tough inferred a number of important conclusions from her data, but two which are of particular interest to educators of young children. She noted first that the more linguistically facile of the children, when given a picture to describe (or, in the case of the very young, peep boxes), tended to begin their discourse from a global or holistic perspective. For example, a picture of a man, woman, and two children in a room with the man reading a newspaper, the woman sewing, the boy playing with a game or toy, and the little girl petting a kitten elicited discourse usually beginning with assertions such as, ''There is a family in a house. This is the father. Here is the mother. These are the children. The daddy has been working . . . [etc.]'' Or, alternatively: ''This is a daddy and mommy and their children are getting ready for dinner . . . [etc.]'' The children begin with the global construct that defines all of the elements in the picture, and then, as their discourse continues, they work their way down to the particular elements of the whole.

On the other hand, less facile language users tend to simply label particulars in the pictures and have to be prodded to articulate further. ''That is a man.'' Pause. The interviewer probes: ''What else is here?'' The child responds with something such as "There is a girl." Again, isolated particulars are often identified rather than the child providing a generalized overview description before elaborating with particulars.

A second and related finding of Tough was that less linguistically capable children tended to use nonelaborated phrases in identifying important features or components of a scene or situation to be described. Generalized pronouns, often lacking specific reference, tended to be used, for example, "It's okay," or "They ran," or "He did it," as opposed to "I liked that girl's pretty blue dress," or "The mean boys with the sack of kittens ran fast," or "The tiny old man with the cane did it."

The ability to elaborate and flesh out information on topics by taking a global approach and then narrowing in and selecting specific descriptor adjectives to extend or qualify noun phrases are abilities unique to the more linguistically expressive and facile. Further, these skills are the kind that tend to be self-reinforcing: They assist directly in the more rapid language development of their users by extending the cognitive range and the kinds of language-using contexts available. In effect, the greater the language facility one possesses, the more likely one is to build from that facility rapidly and effectively.

The discourse (language used in conversational settings) research that examines the oral language use of preschool children indicates other important features of children's language use. For example, we now know that children utilize language for social communicative functions earlier than previously thought and to a greater extent than thought. Piaget had estimated a dominance of egocentric, or self-centered, speech through the preoperational stage of development (to about age 7, although he estimated that even as much as 47 percent of a first-grader's speech could be egocentric).[17] Other continuing research suggests this to be an overestimation of egocentrism and an underestimation of early sophisticated functional uses of language in social contexts.[18] Ongoing research such as this documents children's intentional uses of speech to inform, describe, persuade, manage or control others, and to ritualize.

Most of these uses are employed from 3 years on. Tough even documents children's implicit use of egocentric speech to project next steps in an activity, to plan a long-range strategy, and to control or manipulate the behavior of others![19] Vygotsky's research points significantly to the importance of external speech to the resolution of problems for the young child, even when the problems do not involve others, for example, figuring out how to procure a chocolate bar placed on a high shelf with only a limited supply of tools or aids.[20]

Perhaps of most interest in the area of children's discourse research are the findings of Roger Brown and associates who, after studying the influence of approval and disapproval of their children's talk by parents, concluded:

> There is not a shred of evidence that approval and disapproval are contingent on syntactic correctness. . . . When Eve expressed the opinion that her mother was a girl by saying, "He a girl," her mother answered, "That's right." The child's utterance was ungrammatical, but her mother did not respond to that fact; instead, she responded

to the truth of the proposition the child intended to express. In general, the parent fitted propositions to the child's utterances, and then approved or not according to the correspondence between the proposition and reality. Thus, "Her curl my hair," was approved because the mother was in fact curling Eve's hair. However, Sarah's grammatically impeccable "There's the animal farmhouse," and Adam's "Walt Disney comes on on Tuesday," was disapproved because Walt Disney came on on some other day.[21]

In other words, contrary to some suppositions, parents tend to address the propositional intent of the utterance rather than its grammatical form. Certainly the language environment, as we have noted in research cited earlier, has an important impact on the child; however, the variables that impinge are many and varied. Singling out grammar as a variable for correction bears little promise. In her review of the research in this area, Courtney Cadzen concludes that "evidence on the role of correction in the child's learning of grammar is wholly negative"[22] and that "the implication for education is that teachers may be interfering with the child's learning process by insisting on responses that superficially look or sound 'correct.' "[23] A developmental perspective on the grammar of the child indicates that acceptance of the language of the child and employment of modeling strategies in constructive positive language environments are most conducive to language growth.

In addition to these findings regarding the development of oral language and its use by children as a specific skill area, the educational literature such as the longitudinal studies of Walter Loban suggest important interrelationships among the various language skill areas.[24] And although correlational studies do not necessarily establish cause-effect relationships among factors being considered, they do, when sustained and supported over time with backup research and advocacy from practice, provide a reasonable basis for asserting an instructional rationale. In the case of language skills for children, in both preschool and school-age settings, the literature is replete with common-sense support for the interrelationships among listening, speaking, reading, and writing. Comments such as the following from *Language Arts* (February 1981) are common in the literature: "They [the authors] make clear that interrelated experiences with listening, speaking, reading, writing, art, poetry, and music provide opportunities for everyone to learn language by using language."[25] Or consider: "The quality of children's writing can be little different from the quality of the oral language they use."[26] "Speaking and writing are closely allied arts."[27] "Teachers have always agreed in theory that the skills of oral language were basic to those of reading and writing."[28] "Learning to read and write all depend in large measure on the child's growth in oral speech."[29]

Some authorities such as Patrick Groff have questioned certain of the strong interrelationships among the language skill areas suggested here.[30] However, across the board, in both preschool and school-age settings, the preponderance of support would appear to be in favor of encouraging and capitalizing upon assumed relationships that exist in the various language skill domains.

In the case of preschool children, the central role of oral language and the opportunities to seize upon that language facility are so obvious that the language interrelationships question may be largely irrelevant. We have no choice but to use that resource of the child for building speech skills. In addition, our cultural biases, which have traditionally placed the order of language skills acquisition from listening to speaking to reading to writing, may determine our behavior as much as if not more than any psychological or developmental issues. Whether or not that cultural bias could or should be altered remains to be seen.

GOVERNING PRINCIPLES

After considering the literature of oral language development and its use by children up through the kindergarten years, and in most cases, beyond, it is reasonable to infer a number of important generalizations about that development and use which have implications for the educator. It is from generalizations such as these that techniques and activities for developing language using facility in the child must derive. We also want to assume that the development of written expression in the child is directly related to the effectiveness with which we exploit such generalizations.

Governing Principle 1

The child's oral language in normal development serves as the language base from which all critical language producing and consuming skills derive. By enhancing this language ability, we contribute directly to the prospects of the other language skill areas developing too. Oral language assists directly in the development of intellectual facility, provides a mediating tool for translating experience into reusable form, and provides a critical means for establishing communications with others and, thus, important purposes for the other language skill areas to fulfill. It also provides the essential roots for reading and writing.

This oral language base should be exploited throughout the early childhood years for a variety of reasons, including cognitive development facilitation, as well as for providing a source base for development of related language skills such as reading and writing.

Governing Principle 2

Children learn language meaning as they learn its functions. For the child, language is a tool whose purposes and potential develop in concert with structural and semantic facility. For example, children learn to use the language of direction at the same time they learn that language serves a management and control function. Children as young as three or four use language in cause-effect relationships when the circumstances call for persuasion.

It is important to remember that *it is not difference in language functions that separates the mature from the developing language user so much as it is difference in quality and degree of sophistication.* Young children need to be placed into a variety of communication contexts for a variety of communication purposes and with a variety of audience types throughout their early childhood years. Structuring meaningful talk environments for the child requires parents and teachers who have a sense of the language use types, the communication functions accessible to the child, and a particular sensitivity to the mesh of the two.

Governing Principle 3

The linguistically facile child approaches descriptive and explanatory situations with a capacity to move from a global or holistic assertion of the situation to less abstract and more specific detailed elaboration of the particulars that make up the situation. The opening description or assertion by the speaker or writer establishes the governing character of what is to follow. It provides an organizational mental set the child can use to arrange the details that are to follow. And, although educators cannot nor need not structure the talk circumstances to assure at all times this direction by the child, we do need to take great care to see that there is not an overuse of language activities that encourage labeling, typing, or mere identification with no elaboration, justification, or reinforcing detail provided.

As a general rule, it is useful to keep in mind that form follows function and the particulars within follow form. This is as true in language development as it is in architectural design.

Governing Principle 4

There are strong relationships among the four general language skill areas—speaking, writing, reading, and listening—and given the central role of oral language in the young child, the interrelationships among the skill areas should be encouraged with initial efforts moving from oral language to writing and reading. As development takes place, the movement between can be generated from any one skill area, including writing.

The research suggests that *integrated* language skills development is most desirable. As early as the child can incorporate the natural relationships that exist among the language skill areas in his or her language use, it should be accomplished, and the educator should work toward establishing environments conducive to such integration. When and how written expression should fit into this integration will be considered after we examine the child as writer and handwriter.

THE CHILD AS LINGUIST: WRITER

Jenny, age 6, writes the letter shown in Figure 2–1 to her teacher.

She then reads her letter:

> Dear Ms. Baker,
> I am going to move. I won't be seeing you next week. I hope I'll see you at Christmas. I like you a lot.
> Charley W. [her cat][31]

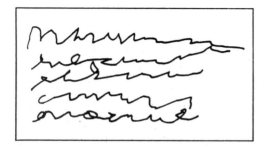

Figure 2-1.

Jenny is learning to write in one sense; in another, she knows how to write and is in the process of refining a skill that she already possesses. We have learned a great deal about how and when children such as Jenny learn to write, as well as its importance to them—despite the fact that research in this area has not been as prolific as in oral language or beginning reading.

A good deal of this research has come from close observation of children in relatively unstructured writing situations,[32] and the data from this research have established a number of important points. Harste and associates, for example, elicited uninterrupted writing samples from three 4-year-olds (see Figure 2–2).

They then talked with the children about their productions. When Najeeba finished writing, she observed, "Here, but you can't read it because it is in Arabic!"[33] Najeeba then pointed out how in Arabic one uses "a lot more dots" than in English. Dalia's writing looks Egyptian enough to be a pyramid inscription.

These three samples offer clear evidence that children early on have a firm grasp of what writing is supposed to look like in respect to its contours and general dimensions. Many American children in the Harste studies gladly read their free-written stories by pointing to the upper left corner and moving the finger along from

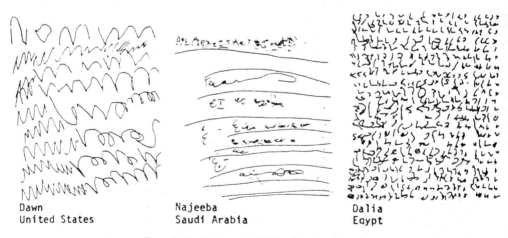

Dawn
United States

Najeeba
Saudi Arabia

Dalia
Egypt

Figure 2–2. Uninterrupted Writing Samples (Age 4).

left to right and from top to bottom, indicating that they also have a grasp for written language's flow, direction, and linearity.

In addition to these discoveries, Harste and associates noted even more sophisticated abilities in young writers. When asked to write both a story and a letter, Megan, age 4, produced the samples shown in Figure 2–3.

Megan's Letter (12/5/78):	"Dear Mary, I would like you to bring bring me . . . here everyday. The end. Megan."
Megan's Story: (12/5/78):	"Once upon a time there was a ghost. Three ghosts family. One day they went out for a walk. They honked the horn cause they saw Mrs. Wood and said 'I' then they went back to Mrs. Corners and they honked the horn and sa-said 'Hi.' The end."

Megan read the two samples to the researcher, as noted above. Notice that her letter includes a heading, body, and signature. Notice also that her story includes the critical structural features of protagonist, antagonist, conflict, resolution, and consequence. Megan is aware of the structural differences in the two modes of discourse and, further, reveals a developing sense that such differences are at least partly reflected in the form and contours of the writing itself.

The efforts of Megan, Dawn, Najeeba, and Dalia suggest to Harste and associates the beginning evolution of a writing system generated partly from writing

Figure 2–3. Megan's Story and Letter: Uninterrupted Writing Samples.

and partly from the children's sociolinguistic environment—writing, print, and other language modes reflected in most of their day-to-day surroundings.

The idea of early writing system employment by children has received a wide range of research support. Research studies by Read and Chomsky have provided clear evidence that young children devise their own spelling system, and, though it is not that of an adult, it is systematic, logical, decodable, and marvelously consistent in its employment.[34] For example, Read observes that children use the letter *a* to represent short *e,* the vowel of *bet* and *red,* more frequently than any other invented spelling, and that young children tend to represent the short *i* of *fish* with an *e.* In other words, children's employment of spelling in the early stages is not totally idiosyncratic. Instead, preschoolers and early-school-age children employ an invented spelling that meets the fundamental rules of any spelling system, except that it doesn't happen to be—yet—that of adult society. Although most children do not come into the adult spelling system until they are of school age, their understanding of its fundamental tenets, contours, purposes, and patterning system develops prior to then.

Applebee, Pitcher and Prelinger, Stein, and others have explored children's perception of sense of story; story grammar; its primary and universal structural components and features, such as the nature of protagonist, antagonist, plot, and conflict resolutions; the order of their appearance; and the network of relationships among them.[35] Applebee notes the initial attributes of this perception at age 2. And he further observes a normal development through the school years, with eventual higher-level sophistication in the later grades. Further, young children can represent the structure of stories.[36] These representations follow a developmental pattern.[37] And the processes involved in representation are quite similar to those of adults.[38] All of these researchers suggest a tacit awareness by children of fundamental story structure to which children pin their own characters and actions as they produce both oral and written narratives. King and Rentel do note, however, that throughout the years, including those of early childhood, considerable differences exist among children in regard to their abilities to recognize and utilize story structure in both spoken and written modes.[39] These differing abilities are highlighted by writing, since it is an abstraction level further removed from the idea than is oral language. And many, such as Vygotsky and Moffett, project that more elaborated narratives in writing are dependent upon inner speech exploitation in a conscious fashion, a cognitive ability beyond the range of most preoperational children (prior to 7 years of age for most). Therefore, intricate elaboration within narrative and the conception of monologue—extended description/narrative—as opposed to dialogue, which is the normal mode of language exchange in the oral world of the young child, is less likely in the very young. And, further, differences in cognitive development may be anticipated to have a significant effect on written expression at these early stages.

These limitations notwithstanding, the young child is able to formulate stories in both oral and written fashion that exhibit critical features common to all major fictional narratives in prose form. He or she is able to do this with no instruction in either formal literacy structures production or in their comprehension.

Indeed, one of the consistent theories that is revealed in the research of those concerned with writing growth is its essential developmental character. The young child grows into and through stages that have particular critical attributes and that themselves prepare the child for the necessary progress through the later stages of development. However, although this characteristic of writing development in children is now widely espoused, there have remained fundamental questions in the minds of researchers. What are these stages that young children go through in their early writing development? What are the salient features of each? What are their indicators?

King and Rentel assert:

> What is needed is a framework for understanding how children's intentions in learning interact with varying learning contexts as they make the transition from speech to writing and, in particular, a framework that focuses on how children *develop* control over the written medium.[40]

In their review of the literature, they note how little attention has been devoted to this area.

DeFord offers an "outline framework" that begins to get at the need identified by King and Rentel:

1. Scribbling
2. Differentiation between drawing and writing
3. Concepts of linearity, uniformity, inner complexity, symmetry, placement, left-to-right motion, and top-to-bottom directionality
4. Development of letters and letter-like shapes
5. Combination of letters, possibly with spaces, indicating understanding of units (letters, words, sentences), but may not show letter sound correspondence
6. Writing known isolated words—developing sound/letter correspondence
7. Writing simple sentences with use of invented spelling
8. Combining two or more sentences to express complete thoughts
9. Control of punctuation—periods, capitalization, use of upper and lower case letters
10. Form of discourse—stories, information material, letters, etc.[41]

This framework, based on a study of children from 2 to 7 years of age, however, describes only the general features of development, and, as DeFord points out, it is not necessarily sequential in its character.

Ironically, considerable work was done in this area in the late 1920s in Russia by Alexander Luria; this work has only recently been translated into English and made available in the West where ongoing similar research is providing substantive elaboration of the stages of writing development in children from 3 to 9 years of age.[42]

Luria was significantly influenced by his mentor, Lev Vygotsky,* particularly with regard to the central role of speech in the development of cognition and the related importance of writing in extending speech potential. Vygotsky argued persuasively that writing was a fundamental assist to cognitive growth as well as a tool for communication. The act of writing and its attendant demands on one's abstracting and symbolizing abilities was to Vygotsky a natural extension of play that served as sort of a preliterate precursor to the more demanding skills of writing. In the evolution of play one can see the child transfer reality from the object world of a hobbyhorse in the form of a stick with head and tail, to the more abstract representations of a plain stick with symbolic power.

This evolution may be seen as a critical first step in the development of a more refined metalinguistic sensitivity that many developmentalists and reading authorities argue is fundamental to the development of the more abstract skills of literacy in reading and writing.[43]

Vygotsky indicated that with this fundamental symbolizing potential the preschool child is quite ready to learn to write and, given the importance of the writing act as cognitive assist, should be taught to write.

> From our point of view, it would be natural to transfer the teaching of writing to the preschool years. Indeed, if younger children are capable of discovering the symbolic function of writing, as Hetzer's experiments have shown, then the teaching of writing should be made the responsibility of pre-school education.[44]

It is, however, Alexander Luria, who, via imaginative descriptive research, provides us with very specific understanding of what children do and go through in the development of written expression, and, more importantly, he shows us that young children do grasp the symbolic functions of writing sooner than we often realize.

Luria begins with the assumption that writing, as is reading, is a culturally mediated function of the individual. And, since writing is a culturally based mediated act, it is reasonable to assume that particular aspects of its development may correspond with features of cultural development as they have shaped our beliefs and behaviors over time. To some extent, this Lurian view may have been derived from political necessity in post–Bolshevik Revolution Russia. Practically, however, it was to serve as a reasonable assumptive base in shaping his methodology for eliciting data from children, for it established a perception of writing development as a process with a "prehistory" and an evolutionary character not unlike that of other social and cultural phenomena. As cultures go through stages of development, so too do children in the development of written expression. Luria's work elaborates those stages, their characteristics, and their importance for the child.

One must remember, according to Luria, that the ability to write presupposes that the child is already capable of differentiating relationships among the various

---

*Luria once observed regarding his own work: "After more than half a century in science I am unable to name another person who even approaches his [Vygotsky's] incredible analytic ability and foresight. All of my work has been no more than the working out of the psychological theory which he constructed." From L. S. Vygotsky, *Mind in Society.*

elements of the object world. The child must be able to utilize various social "tools" to do this differentiating. Initially the child relies on physical objects to serve in this differentiating role; toys, sticks, and other material objects. This prehistory period of crude differentiating gives way to the more highly refined social instruments of play and language to achieve the same purposes. The ultimate critical discovery for the child, of course, is that language, as an auxiliary device, has the symbolizing and abstracting potential to transcend time and space as well as material reality. Once this discovery is made, then writing can flourish.

Luria's search for insights into how and when the transition from prehistory to writing takes place was governed by an experimental methodology that presupposed an evolutionary character in the acquisition of the writing act as a symbolizing and mediating one divorced from the material events being represented. He further assumed that the easiest way to proceed was to ask the child to remember a series of sentences or phrases and clauses by utilizing paper and pencil. When responding, as they often did, that they couldn't write, the children were encouraged to use the provided materials in any way that would help them to remember.

Children were presented with six to eight sentences (also phrases and clauses)—usually short, simple, and unrelated—and they were asked to remember them. Luria then carefully analyzed responses to the task by children from 3 to 9 years of age.

Initial work with 3-, 4-, and 5-year-olds suggested that most of these children did not perceive writing as a mediating act of any kind. Many grasped its outward forms with some sense of how adults do it. Some could even do a reasonable job of imitating adult writing. However, for most, it was purely imitative and nonmediated. For example, Vova (5 years old), in response to the request to remember and write down "Mice have long tails," made a number of scrawls and responded, "That's how you write" (see Figure 2–4).

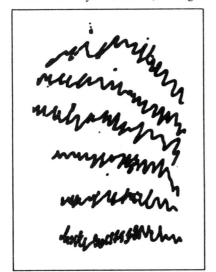

Figure 2–4.

In fact, many children at this stage simply began scrawling figures or lines before instructions were given and continued after the experiment was completed. Further, when asked to use the scrawls as a mnemonic device, they couldn't do it. The "writing" served no instrumental or functional role. This was the case even for many kindergarten children. They love to scribble simply for fun in this sort of task but fail to grasp the instrumental potential of writing as a linguistic tool.

Luria refers to this first stage as the Pre-writing, or Pre-instrumental, Phase. It can extend for several years from ages three through five, but there are a number of dynamic factors that serve to warn against making sharp or refined connections between age and stage in early writing development. Luria did note that, when asked to write, children in this stage used scrawls in zigzag, straight-line form (see Figure 2–5).

When asked to write with signs, the same child converted from marks that closely resemble adult writing to marks such as those in Figure 2–6. Despite uniqueness of form, they, too, are random, undifferentiated, and reflect no mnemonic potential. Children are unable to use these marks mnemonically, just as

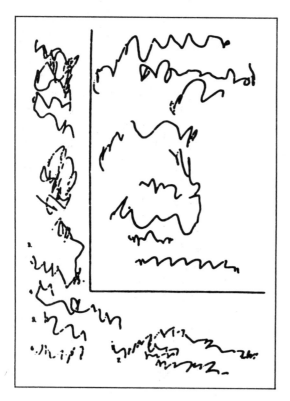

Figure 2–5.

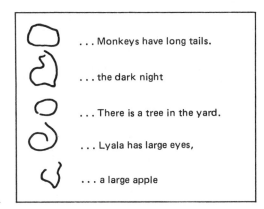

... Monkeys have long tails.

... the dark night

... There is a tree in the yard.

... Lyala has large eyes,

... a large apple

Figure 2–6.

they were unable to use the other scrawls. In fact, in this stage the child is often better able to recall the given information when he or she has attempted to write nothing. The writing attempts often interfere with retention of the information. And, when children do recall the information after writing, they do not use the scrawls on paper as cues. They often stare out of the window or at the ceiling, indicating that the recall process was largely unrelated to any possible meaning retention cued by marks on paper. At most, children remembered only two or three sentences or phrases at this stage.

Progress to the second stage of writing development, the differentiating phase, comes when the child perceives some differentiation potential in the writing. This is reflected in two ways. The first is in an attempt to intentionally build in some outward correspondence between quantity and rhythm of the utterance and a preservation of that in the written expression. The child simply begins to show a tendency to write down given words or short phrases with short lines and longer words, phrases, and/or sentences with longer lines or a larger number of scribbles.

Perhaps the most dramatic discovery Luria made in his research came next. He discovered that utilization of numbers, or quantification, in language could serve as a powerful assist in moving the young child into the differentiated stage of written expression development. Luria asserts:

> By introducing the factor of number into the material, we could readily produce differentiated graphic activity in 4–5 year-old children by causing them to use signs to reflect this number. It is possible that the actual origins of writing are to be found in the need to record number, or quantity.[45]

For example, in a first session Brina (5 years) had five sentences dictated to her: (1) the bird is flying, (2) the elephant has a long trunk, (3) an automobile goes fast, (4) there are high waves on the sea, and (5) the dog barks. The subject drew separate lines in columns but recalled only two of the sentences, the same number she recalled without any use of pen and paper. In later sessions she was given syntactic constructs with quantification, for example, a man has two arms, the big dog has four pups, Brina has 20 teeth. By the fourth session, she could recall virtually all of the material, missing on only one if at all. Further, her written expression technique was altered to incorporate the quantification factor in some way, often by separate marks corresponding to the numbers given in the phrase or sentence. For example, she represented "A man has two arms and two legs" with two separate marks or lines. A similar result was obtained from a wide range of subjects in Luria's work. For the first time, then, the child *intentionally* employs written expression for mnemonic purposes. It thus serves an explicit symbolic role.

A second "stimulator" of differentiated graphic activity for mnemonic cueing is seen in protocols that employ color as a modifier of key nominals. For example, "Very black smoke is coming from the chimney," or "The snow was very soft and white." In the "smoke" example, children often drew heavy dark marks with comments such as "Black—like this!"

The child preserves quantification by converting the scrawls or marks to numerical indicators. The child preserves modification-by-color by altering the intensity of the written form itself. In both techniques the written expression serves a distinct mnemonic role for the child; the written expression performs a mediating function and facilitates recall. Both quantification and form assume a critical role in moving the child to pictography as the final step before the child finally addresses the ideographic role of written language in symbolic form.

Luria's data strongly suggest that throughout the writing development process there is a general progression from the first undifferentiated phase to and through pictography to the final stage of ideography where the child understands and exploits the symbolic potential of language. Writing development, however, does not progress in a consistent "straight line." As with other cultural phenomena there is a plateauing for brief periods; there is backtracking; there is a zigzag sort of movement where children appear, temporarily at least, to regress. Luria's observations regarding the initial difficulty the child has in mastering the various facilities of the differentiated stage of writing development, in many senses, serve as precursors to later, in fact much more recent, research into the acquisition and attendant complexities of metalinguistic awareness, that is, the ability to see language as a construct or system in itself as well as a means for communicating with another. For example, Vasya G., a 6-year-old boy who was a typical respondent, knew the individual letters *A* and *I*. When asked to remember and write some dictated sentences, he easily employed the letters he knew, but quite arbitrarily it turns out. For, when asked to read the sentences back, he simply read the letters *A* and *I* as he had previously used them.

The child at this stage relates quite externally to writing as a mediating process. Understanding of the mechanisms of writing takes place after the outward mastery of those behaviors many of us would accept as performance indicators of one's knowledge of writing. The child understands that he can use signs to write with before he understands how to use them!

The beginning writer, according to Luria, assimilates experience through writing in a purely external fashion initially. Then the writer comes to realize and utilize the powerful potential of writing as symbolic expressive behavior. And it is in this order of evolution that Luria finds critical significance. For, in Luria's words, *"It is not understanding that generates the act, but far more the act that gives birth to understanding—indeed, the act often far precedes understanding."*[46] Prior to a conceptualization of writing as a symbolic process with abstracting power, the child goes through an evolutionary prehistory of writing that, while crude, exhibits every indication of contributing to the ultimate expressive facility that later appears.

Luria's work suggests that we need to reexamine in serious fashion our current conceptions about when and how to begin writing instruction with children. He offers persuasive evidence that considerable learning potential remains unrealized in preschool children. Three-, 4-, and 5-year-olds are already in the evolutionary process of writing development in literate societies often long before many of us would have assumed.

Luria's elaboration of the writing stage evolvement from undifferentiated to differentiated—with quantification and form representing potential instructional assists—and his insightful findings revealing the movement of the child within the differentiated stage of development from pictography to ideography could have dramatic implications for curriculum and instruction design during the formative years of preschool and the early primary grades.

GOVERNING PRINCIPLES

An examination of the research and theory literature that addresses early writing in children provides us with the following set of governing principles for shaping instructional decisions in early childhood education.

Governing Principle 1

Writing acquisition is a developmental process for the preschool child beginning essentially around 3+ years of age. This developmental process appears to evolve in a regular and reasonably systematic fashion that eventually leads the child to an appreciation of writing-as-conceptual-act.

Governing Principle 2

The stages of writing development have been identified according to varying frameworks of stage types. The most thoroughly elaborated model is that of Alexander Luria, which specifies four distinct but overlapping stages: (1) undifferentiated (ages 3 to 5); (2) differentiated (ages 4 to 6); (3) pictographic (ages 4 to 6); and (4) ideographic (ages 4 to 9).

These stages, again, are *not* solely a function of age. There is a general movement from 1 through 4. However, between 3 and 6 years of age it is quite common to find children of the same age two or three stages apart from each other.

Further, there appears to be every reason to assume that occasional movement backward—what might appear to be regression—is quite normal in given contexts or situations where a child is asked to cope with an unusual or demanding writing task or problem. This is particularly conspicuous between the pictographic and ideographic stages.

Governing Principle 3

Most children intuitively know the fundamental contours of writing, its linearity, basic dimensions, as well as its general societal role for adults, before they possess the fine motor skills necessary to produce accessible written expression and before they have the cognitive ability to grasp its symbolic and abstract character. The prehistory of writing is substantively tied to critical developments that occur in the child's evolving conception of play and recognition of the potential of oral language for serving critical cognitive nonverbal tasks. One of the most fundamental of the many roles served by play in the life of the child is its role in helping the child conceptualize symbol as a relatively abstract entity capable of being utilized for purposes other than its initial object reality appearance suggests. Early scribble writing and mark making on paper or chalkboard fall within the rubric of "language play" and are a critical part of this prehistory phase of writing development.

This concept of language play also refers to that occurring in oral language. Children exploit such avenues as riddles, puns, jokes, nonsense rhymes and street chants in the writing prehistory phase and even throughout the writing development stages to enhance their developing metalinguistic awareness, an awareness that ultimately proves to be essential to all literacy skills.

Governing Principle 4

Children reflect an intuitive grasp of the basic structures of story grammar at the ages of 2 and 3. They employ this sense of structure in understanding stories read to them and in reproducing their own in written expression. It is also reasonable to assume that this is one area where language consumption (listening and reading) and language production (speaking and writing) directly assist each other and the individual employing these skills. This sense of story grammar and its more sophisticated attributes continue to develop through the early childhood, intermediate childhood, and middle school years. This is an important concept for the child's writing development in two ways. First, a grasp of story grammar provides an initial framework—mental outline, if you will—for the child to hang written expression on in creating writing. Second, and perhaps even more important, sense of story grammar implicitly directs the child's attention to the more global rhetorical concepts that are central to all writing—unity, coherence, organization, development, transition, and style. All of the concepts that the child will hopefully master in later writing have their fundamental roots in the sense of structure in stories—an intuitive given for the child in its most basic form!

THE CHILD AS LINGUIST: HANDWRITER

Normally handwriting is an area reserved for treatment with the *school-age* child, since instruction seldom begins prior to kindergarten in most formal programs. There is, however, a considerable body of research and theory interest in areas often referred to as "prehandwriting" or "handwriting readiness." And, most educators recognize the area, regardless of its label, as an important one and one that is formative for later practices and behaviors of the child.

Although there is not complete concurrence on what skills constitute "prehandwriting," there is reasonable agreement on what the categories of important skills probably are. Lamme identifies six such categories as "prerequisite skill areas for handwriting": small muscle development (fine motor skill), eye-hand coordination, holding a writing tool, basic strokes, letter perception, and orientation to printed language.[47]

Development of small muscles (fine motor) and related eye-hand coordination has a longstanding tradition of advocacy in education for a variety of reasons, including handwriting readiness development. Recent developmental psychologists and early childhood educators even argue substantively for preschool programs based on physical activities essential to cognitive growth.[48] Regardless of whether one concurs with this position, certainly activities designed to enhance small muscle development and eye-hand coordination are widely regarded as important. Reasonable expectations in fine motor development have been proposed by Maxim:

AGE	FINE MOTOR ABILITIES
1–2 years	Can hold pencil or crayon
	Can pull off shoes and socks
	Can begin to drink from a cup and feed themselves with a spoon
2–3 years	Can scribble with pencil or crayons
	Can open boxes and other simple containers
	Can begin to use knives and forks when feeding themselves
3–4 years	Can use pencils or crayons to copy circles or simple lines
	Can print large capital letters
	Can use modeling clay, make cookies, and sew
	Can feed themselves well and wash and dry dishes
4–6 years	Can copy some simple geometric figures
	Can print their names, the entire alphabet, and number from 1 to 20
	Can build crude models from wood and other materials
	Can bathe themselves, brush their own teeth and hair
	Can dress themselves completely, except for tying shoes.[49]

A cursory glance at Maxim's expectations reveals many abilities that clearly go beyond prehandwriting and into handwriting itself.

And, just as it is difficult to separate entirely those skills that are "prehand-writing" from those that constitute "handwriting," it is also quite difficult to distinguish between fine motor (small muscle) skills and eye-hand coordination skills. What some authorities treat as one type others prefer to think of as the other. Certainly it is difficult to think of a fine motor activity or skill that does not also involve to a significant extent eye-hand coordination.

And so it is with the other skill categories, whether they be Lamme's or someone else's. Without undue concern for the skill category classification, howev-er, we can note some significant research findings in this entire area of handwriting readiness or, if one prefers, initial handwriting.

Although there is some historical precedent for advocating larger than normal-sized writing instruments for younger children, recent research suggests this to be unnecessary, if not undesirable. Freeman, Taylor, West, and McKee also advocate initial instruction at the chalkboard prior to use of pen and pencil.[50] There has been no substantial research support for these early positions on handwriting instruction, however. Wiles, studying 800 first-graders, found no justification for special-sized writing instruments.[51] And Tawney and Kryesni found that children in the primary grades do as well with ballpoint pens as with pencils.[52] Krzesni suggests space between lines is also not a critical matter, as do Halpin and Halpin.[53]

Positions on initial writing utensils for preschool children vary somewhat. Lamme asserts that there is a hierarchy of difficulty in writing utensils, the pencil being the most difficult, therefore the last that should be given to the child.[54] Others conclude: "Until further evidence is available, it appears satisfactory to allow beginning writers to select and use the tools they find comfortable for manipulation and control."[55] Similar positions abound in the literature on early handwriting practice, that is, to the effect that one should provide a variety of colorful and imaginative writing materials and equipment for the child to choose from.

Those who question the ability of the preschooler to master any essential handwriting skills should consider Maria Montessori's instructional program. Maria Montessori was a strong advocate of early handwriting in the preschool;

> Why should we not write independently of such analysis? . . . (referring to ability to analyze letters and their use) It would be sad indeed if we could *speak* only *after* we had studied grammar! It would be much the same as demanding before we looked at the stars in the firmament, we must study infinitesimal calculus; it is much the same to feel that before teaching an idiot to write, we must make him understand the abstract derivation of lines and the problem of geometry!
>
> No less are we to be pitied if, in order to write, we must follow analytically the parts constituting the alphabetical signs.[56]

Montessori's early handwriting program emphasized the natural development of the child. Prewriting activities focusing upon small muscle development and eye-hand coordination make effective use of sensory experiences—sewing and weaving, for example. She then taught letter recognition and formation, using templates and tracing of letter contours with finger tips on rough textured boards and similar devices. Montessori argued that this facilitated *muscular memory*.

Montessori suggested her techniques led children to an interest in writing by 4 years of age and some "writing" as early as 3½ years. Although not necessarily typical, the writing sample by a 5-year-old shown in Figure 2–7 gives some indication of handwriting potential in preschoolers.

Montessori utilized both copying and tracing activities in her approach to initial handwriting instruction. However, research by Hirsch and Niedermeyer and by Askov and Greff indicate that copying of letter shapes is more effective than tracing for initial instruction.[57] Foerster suggests that tracing focuses attention on the mechanics of letter parts rather than the more global contours of letters or words.[58] The most widely accepted approaches appear to be those reflecting variety, adequate creative and colorful materials and utensils, and sensitivity to the child's cognitive, physical, and emotional readiness.

Wright and Allen suggest practice in basic strokes, as in Figure 2–8, as part of the prehandwriting phase.[59] This, in fact, is often suggested by early childhood educators.[60] However, there is considerable variety in the methodologies advocated, ranging from formal drill to informal practice in sand or finger painting.

The relationships that hold between drawing and handwriting are obvious. Luria, in fact, establishes a fundamental role for pictography, you will recall, in the development of writing-as-conceptual-act in the child, the mechanics of the process aside. Many educators note that the employment of basic strokes in one form or another is an indicator of readiness to begin formal handwriting instruction. And the

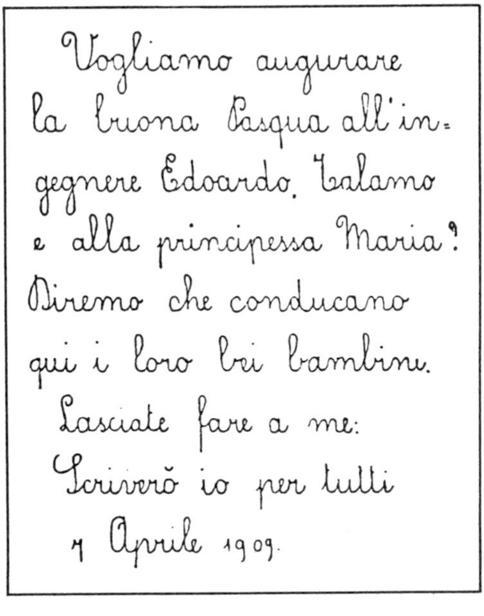
Vogliamo augurare
la buona Pasqua all'in=
gegnere Edoardo. Talamo
e alla principessa Maria!
Diremo che conducano
qui i loro bei bambini.
Lasciate fare a me:
Scriverò io per tutti
7 Aprile 1909.

Figure 2–7. Example of writing done with pen and ink by a child of 5 years. Translation: "We would like to wish a joyous Easter to the civil engineer Edoardo Talamo and the Princess Maria. We will ask them to bring their pretty children here. Leave it to me: I will write for all. April 7, 1909." (Reproduced by permission of Schocken Books, Inc., New York, N.Y., from *The Montessori Method* by Maria Montessori, 1964.)

art work of the child is suggested as one means for assessing skills in the nine basic strokes (see Figure 2–8).

$$/ - \backslash /\ O \supset \cap \cup \cap$$

Figure 2–8.

Some authorities advise that children at levels *d* and *e* of Figure 2–9 are ready for beginning handwriting instruction, while the producers of the other three drawings probably are not. However, it would appear more reasonable to make judgments about readiness with both more comprehensive and more global criteria than basic strokes alone. Clay recommends the following:

Recurring principle—the child repeats patterns (or letters or words) over and over.

Directional principle—the child goes from left to right and then return sweeps to begin again at the left.

Generating principle—the child realizes that letter elements can recur in variable patterns.

Inventory principle—the child lists all of the letters (or words or symbols) he or she knows.

Contrastive principle—the child perceives likenesses and differences among letter elements, concepts, letters, and words.[61]

There is general acceptance of the position that knowing the alphabet is not a skill prerequisite to handwriting although an ability to recognize letters of the alphabet may be. Lewis and Lewis contend that there is an order of difficulty in alphabet letter production for children that includes both capital and small letters.[62] The following tabulation shows the Lewises' specific conclusions, with letters ordered from most to least difficult:

1. q	14. U	27. K	40. F
2. g	15. M	28. W	41. P
3. p	16. S	29. A	42. E
4. y	17. b	30. N	43. X
5. j	18. e	31. C	44. I
6. m	19. r	32. f	45. v
7. k	20. z	33. J	46. i
8. u	21. n	34. W	47. D
9. a	22. S	35. h	48. H
10. G	23. Q	36. T	49. O
11. R	24. B	37. x	50. L
12. d	25. t	38. c	51. o
13. Y	26. z	39. V	52. l

A short perusal suggests that the "descenders"—final structure dropping below the line after initial curved or angled configurations—are the most difficult letters to form, while the circle and straight-line contoured letters remain the easiest. We

a

Only a suggestion of form is evident; many details are missing; control of crayon is erratic.

b

Lack of perception of the relationship of the parts to the whole is apparent; details are missing; some details are overelaborated.

c

Keener observation of form is noticeable; significant details are included, such as ears, arms, hands; hair placement is more accurate.

d

An awareness of the relationship of the parts to the whole is shown; many details such as eyebrows, fingers, neck, and shoulders are included; broad strokes of the crayon are used consistently.

e

An understanding of body proportions is revealed; a variety of details makes a realistic picture; good crayon manipulation is evident.

Figure 2–9. Forms drawn by children at various stages of maturity. (From *Handwriting in Kindergarten*, Seattle Public Schools, Seattle, Wa., 1978. Used with permission.)

should note, too, however, that the Lewis and Lewis study dealt with first-grade children. Hence, preschoolers may reasonably be expected to reflect even more difficulty in producing the letters free style in a "classroom-acceptable fashion."

A commonly espoused prerequisite ability for initial handwriting instruction is letter perception and word perception abilities. Recent research revealing the relatively late acquisition of metalinguistic abilities in primary grade children would suggest that letter or word perception as fundamental to beginning handwriting must be seen in a very general way. Many children in the second grade—children already reading and writing—often lack metalinguistic abilities. We have strong reason to believe in fact that children need not have a metalinguistic grasp of letter and word in order to begin handwriting. Perhaps more importantly, handwriting, taught from a language-based perspective, may contribute to the development of metalinguistic awareness.

What appears to be most critical in this entire arena of writing/handwriting/prehandwriting is that no significant portion of any instruction should be taught in a context devoid of a communication purpose that is both meaningful and important to the child.

The child must learn writing-as-conceptual-act and writing-as-mechanical-process in order to use the skills associated with written language. Isolating either notion from the other is setting the child up for unnecessary frustrations in learning this most important language skill area.

GOVERNING PRINCIPLES

The following governing principles regarding instruction in "handwriting readiness" are intended to supplement those discussed in the previous section on "writing."

Governing Principle 1

The distinctions between "prehandwriting," "handwriting readiness," and "handwriting" instruction are not at all clear. This entire arena of instruction should be seen as a continuum of growth that begins in the preschool setting and then carries into the formal school years.

Governing Principle 2

Decisions regarding initial instruction for pre-K or kindergarten children in prehandwriting must be made only after careful consideration of the physical, cognitive, and emotional readiness of the child. Research and practical evidence suggests that by age 4, and for many 3-year-olds, a variety of activities can be undertaken to teach important prehandwriting skills. However, careful informal assessment of children's fine motor skills and general cognitive and emotional readiness ought to be done before utilizing techniques and activities we normally perceive as prehandwriting-related.

Governing Principle 3

Activities and materials designed to teach prehandwriting skills to the preschool or kindergarten child should derive from an overall rationale for instruction that recognizes the importance of creativity, physical appeal, variety and flexibility in approach, and that accommodates young children's needs and abilities. A wide variety and range of abilities will already be reflected in children from 3 years on up. Initial instruction should be open, largely unstructured (with regard to skill categories such as basic strokes), and self-directed by the child, choosing from various writing utensils and/or other materials designed to teach fine motor skills and eye-hand coordination.

Governing Principle 4

Handwriting and writing are two skills that are related but are also unrelated. Handwriting is a mechanical performance skill whose only role is to make writing decipherable. Learning how to handwrite does not *teach the child how to write, how to compose language and express ideas, or how to master writing-as-conceptual-act.* The child has an implicit desire to express self and to express feelings and ideas to others. Writing-as-conceptual-act then must be developed either in concert with or prior to writing-as-mechanical-process. Given these two options, it would appear most desirable for educators of young children to develop *both* of these facilities in tandem, in conjunction with each other. The result then will be children who know how, what, and why to write as well as how to express that writing in a decipherable fashion.

NOTES

1. J. C. Harste and R. F. Carey, "Classroom Constraints and the Language Process" (unpublished manuscript, Indiana University, 1979).

2. Ibid.

3. L. Bloom, *One Word at a Time* (The Hague: Mouton and Company, 1975).

4. M. Klein, *Talk in The Language Arts Classroom* (Urbana, Ill.: National Council of Teachers of English and ERIC/RCS, 1977).

5. P. Menyuk, *Sentences Children Use* (Cambridge: MIT Press, 1969).

6. M. K. Halliday, *Explorations in The Functions of Language* (London: Edward Arnold, 1973); M. K. Halliday, "Learning How to Mean," in *Foundations of Language Development,* Vol. 1, eds., E. H. and E. Lenneberg (New York: Academic Press, 1975); J. Tough, *Focus on Meaning* (London: George Allen and Unwin Ltd., 1973); J. Tough, *The Development of Meaning* (New York: John

Wiley, 1977); and B. Fillion, F. Smith, and M. Swain, "Language 'Basics' for Language Teachers: Towards a Set of Universal Considerations," *Language Arts,* 53 (October 1976): 740–45.

7. Klein, *Talk in The Language Arts Classroom;* M. Klein, "Language and the Child: A Few Key Generalizations," *Educational Leadership* (March 1981); R. Brown, *A First Language: The Early Stages* (Cambridge: Harvard University Press, 1973); C. Cazden, ed., *Child Language and Education* (New York: Holt, Rinehart & Winston, 1972); and P. Dale, *Language Development: Structure and Function* (New York: Holt, Rinehart & Winston, 1976).

8. J. Piaget, *The Language and Thought of The Child* (New York: The Humanities Press, 1959).

9. Dale, *Language Development.*

10. Menyuk, *Sentences Children Use;* C. Reed, ed., *The Learning of Language* (Urbana, Ill.: NCTE, 1971); and Cazden, *Child Language and Education.*

11. C. Snow and C. Ferguson, eds., *Talking to Children* (Cambridge: Cambridge University Press, 1977).

12. L. Vygotsky, *Mind in Society* (Cambridge: Harvard University Press, 1978), p. 27.

13. Ibid., p. 33.

14. Ibid., pp. 25–26.

15. W. Rupley and M. Russell, "The Interaction of Language, Cognitive, and Social Development" *Language Arts* (September 1979), pp. 697–99.

16. Tough, *The Development of Meaning;* Tough, *Focus on Meaning.*

17. Piaget, *The Language and Thought of the Child.*

18. L. Vygotsky, *Thought and Language* (Cambridge: MIT Press, 1962); Vygotsky, *Mind in Society;* Tough, *Focus on Meaning;* Tough, *The Development of Meaning;* Snow and Ferguson, *Talking to Children;* S. Ervin-Tripp and C. Mitchell-Kernan, eds., *Child Discourse* (New York: Academic Press, 1977); J. Gumperz and D. Hymes, eds., *Directions in Sociolinguistics* (New York: Holt, Rinehart & Winston, 1972); P. M. Greenfield and J. H. Smith, *The Structure of Communication in Early Language Development* (New York: Academic Press, 1976); N. B. Jones, *Ethological Studies in Child Behavior* (Cambridge: Cambridge University Press, 1972); and K. Nelson, ed., *Children's Language: Volume I* (New York: Gardner Press, 1978).

19. Tough, *The Development of Meaning.*

20. Vygotsky, *Mind in Society.*

21. Brown and others, in *Child Language and Education,* ed. C. Cazden (New York: Holt, Rinehart & Winston, 1972).

22. Cazden, ed., *Child Language and Education,* p. 111.

23. Ibid.

24. W. Loban, *The Language of Elementary School Children* (Urbana, Ill.: NCTE, 1963); W. Loban, *Language Development: Kindergarten Through Grade 12* (Urbana, Ill.: NCTE, 1976); E. Thorn, *Teaching and the Language Arts* (Toronto: Gage Publishing, 1974); H. Newman, "Interrelationships of the Language Arts

in the Classroom,'' in *Elementary School Language Arts: Selected Readings*, eds. P. Burns and L. Schell (Chicago: Rand McNally & Company, 1973); and D. Strickland, ''The Language of Elementary School Children: Its Relationship to the Language of Reading Textbooks and the Quality of Reading of Selected Children,'' *Bulletin of The School of Education* (Indiana University, July 1962).

25. J. Jensen, ''Opening Remarks Column,'' *Language Arts* (February 1981), 145.

26. H. K. Macintosh, ed., *Children and Oral Language* (Washington, D.C.: Association of Childhood Education International, 1964).

27. D. H. Russell, ed., *Child Development and the Language Arts* (Champaign, Ill.: NCTE, 1953).

28. W. M. Possien, ed., *They All Need to Talk* (New York: Appleton-Century-Crofts, 1969).

29. J. Moffett, *A Student-Centered Language Arts Curriculum, Grades K–6: A Handbook for Teachers* (Boston: Houghton Mifflin, 1973).

30. P. Groff, ''Oral Language and Reading,'' *Reading World* (October 1977), 71–78; and P. Groff, ''Children's Oral Language and Their Written Composition,'' *The Elementary School Journal* (January 1978), 181–91.

31. D. DeFord, ''Young Children and Their Writing,'' in *Learning to Write: An Expression of Language*, ed. D. DeFord (Columbus: The Ohio State University, Summer 1980), pp. 157–62.

32. Harste and Carey, ''Classroom Constraints and the Language Process''; J. Harste and C. Burke, ''Examining Instructional Assumptions: The Child As Informant,'' in *Learning to Write: An Expression of Language*, ed. D. DeFord (Columbus: The Ohio State University, Summer 1980), 170–78; M. Clay, *What Did I Write?* (Aukland, New Zealand: Heinemann, 1975); and DeFord, ''Young Children and Their Writing,'' pp. 157–62.

33. J. Harste, C. Burke, and V. Woodward, ''Children, Their Language and World: Initial Encounters with Print'' (unpublished manuscript, 1979).

34. C. Read, ''Children's Judgments of Phonetic Similarities in Relation to English Spelling,'' *Language Learning, 23* (June 1973): 17–38; C. Chomsky, ''Education, Writing and Phonology,'' *Harvard Educational Review*, 40 (1970): 287–309; and C. Read, ''What Children Know About Language: Three Examples,'' *Language Arts* (February 1980), 144–48.

35. A. Applebee, *The Child's Concept of Story: Ages Two to Seventeen* (Chicago: University of Chicago Press, 1978); E. Pitcher and E. Prelinger, *Children Tell Stories* (New York: International University Press, 1963); N. Stein, ''How Children Understand Stories: A Developmental Analysis,'' Center for the Study of Reading, University of Illinois at Urbana-Champaign, *Tech. Report* 69 (March 1978); M. King, ''Learning How to Mean in Written Language,'' in *Learning to Write*, ed. DeFord, pp. 163–69; Vygotsky, *Thought and Language;* Vygotsky, *Mind in Society;* and Moffett, *A Student-Centered Language Arts Curriculum.*

36. J. M. Mandler and M. S. Johnson, ''Remembrance of Things Past: Story Structure and Recall,'' *Cognitive Psychology*, 9 (1977): 111–51.

37. A. Applebee, *The Child's Concept of Story*, and G. Brown, ''Children's

Sense of Story in Relation to Reading and Writing'' (unpublished Master's thesis, The Ohio State University, 1977).

38. R. Dungan, ''Prose Memory of Good and Poor First Grade Readers: Effects of Repeated Exposures'' (unpublished Doctoral dissertation, The Ohio State University, 1977).

39. M. King and V. Rentel, ''Toward a Theory of Early Writing Development,'' *Research in the Teaching of English,* 13 (October 1979): 243–53.

40. Ibid.

41. D. DeFord, ''Young Children and Their Writing,'' pp. 157–62.

42. A. Luria, ''The Development of Writing in the Child,'' *Soviet Psychology,* 16 (Winter 1977/78): 65–113.

43. J. Downing and P. Oliver, ''The Child's Conception of 'A Word,' '' *Reading Research Quarterly,* 9 (1974): 568–82; I. Papandropoulou and H. Sinclair, ''What Is a Word?'' *Human Development,* 17 (1977): 257–81; and A. Sinclair, W. Jarvella, and W. Levelt, eds., *The Child's Conception of Language* (Berlin: Springer-Verloz, 1978).

44. Vygotsky, *Mind in Society,* p. 116.

45. Luria, ''The Development of Writing in the Child,'' p. 87.

46. Ibid., p. 113.

47. L. Lamme, ''Handwriting in an Early Childhood Curriculum,'' *Young Children,* 35 (November 1979): 20–27.

48. E. Kamii and R. DeVries, *Physical Knowledge in Preschool Education: Implications of Piaget's Theory* (Englewood Cliffs: Prentice-Hall, 1978).

49. G. Maxim, *The Very Young: Guiding Children from Infancy Through the Early Years* (Belmont, Calif.: Wadsworth, 1980).

50. F. Freeman, *The Zaner-Bloser Correlated Handwriting* (Columbus: The Zaner-Bloser Company, 1936); J. S. Taylor, *Supervision and Teaching of Handwriting* (Richmond: Johnson Publishing Company, 1926); P. V. West, *Changing Practice in Handwriting Instruction* (Bloomington, Ill.: Public School Publishing, 1927); and P. McKee, *Language in the Elementary School* (New York: Houghton Mifflin Company, 1934).

51. M. Wiles, *The Effects of Different Sizes of Tools upon the Handwriting of Beginners* (unpublished Doctoral dissertation, Harvard University, 1940).

52. S. Tawney, ''An Analysis of the Ball Point Pen Versus the Pencil as a Beginning Handwriting Instrument,'' *Elementary English* (January 1967).

53. J. S. Krzesni, ''Effect of Different Writing Tools and Paper on Performance of the Third Grade,'' *Elementary English* (November 1971); G. Halpin and G. Halpin, ''Special Paper for Beginning Handwriting: An Unjustified Practice?'' *Journal of Educational Research,* 69 (1976): 267–69.

54. Lamme, ''Handwriting in an Early Childhood Curriculum,'' pp. 20–27.

55. T. Yawkey and others, *Language Arts and The Young Child* (Itasca, Ill.: Peacock Publishers, 1981).

56. Reprinted by permission of Schocken Books Inc. from *The Montessori Method* by Maria Montessori. Copyright © 1964 by Schocken Books Inc.

57. E. Hirsch and F. C. Niedermeyer, "The Effects of Tracing Prompts and Discrimination training on Kindergarten Handwriting Performance," *Journal of Educational Research,* 67 (1973): 81–86; and E. Askov and E. Greff, "Handwriting: Copying Versus Tracing as the Most Effective Type of Practice," *Journal of Educational Research,* 69 (1975): 96–98.

58. L. Foerster, "Teacher—Don't Let Your First Graders Trace!" *Elementary English,* 49 (1972): 431–33.

59. J. Wright and E. G. Allen, "Ready to Write!" *The Elementary School Journal,* 75 (1975): 430–35.

60. Maxim, *The Very Young: Guiding Children from Infancy Through the Early Years;* and T. Yawkey and others, *Language Arts and the Young Child.*

61. M. Clay, *What Did I Write?*

62. E. R. Lewis and H. P. Lewis, "Which Manuscript Letters are Hard for First Graders?" *Elementary English,* 41 (December 1964): 855–58.

Helping the
Preschool/Kindergarten
Child Develop
Writing Abilities

chapter
3

In this chapter we shall consider a variety of materials, approaches to, and activities for teaching writing and handwriting to preschool through kindergarten children. These ideas will incorporate the three general language areas that were covered in Chapter 2—oral language, writing, and handwriting. It should be recognized immediately, however, that these categories are not to be perceived as separate and distinct from one another. That is neither possible nor desirable. We have argued at some length, for example, for the critical role of oral language as the base from which writing grows. We have also argued that many activities and materials are designed to capitalize upon the ties that relate the various language skills to one another. Therefore, it should be obvious that the placement of many activities, techniques, or strategies is at times arbitrary. This should be of little concern to us, however, for applicability is the primary objective here. The activities, techniques, and strategies will be clustered within three major areas of writing development, namely, oral language, foundation skills, and symbol development.

EXPLOITING ORAL LANGUAGE

Exploiting is a term intended here in a positive sense. We mean by *exploitation* that the skill potential of the child should be drawn out and capitalized upon by the teacher. The language resources the child possesses should be used by the child.

There are three major oral language use types necessary to tap. One is narration. Narrative is the language of story telling and elaborating. For young as well as older children, it is an especially critical area of language exploitation. A second language use type is exposition. Expository language is the language of description and explanation. When reporting on how to assemble a toy or describing (telling about) a trip to the store, the child employs expository uses of language. And a third type is persuasion, or using language to convince another of a point or issue. The ability to argue persuasively is an important skill to develop.

All three of these language use types appear in both oral and written form. And, although there are significant differences between oral and written language, the modes of discourse are the same in each—narration, exposition, and persuasion. Employing these modes for meaningful purposes will help the young child come to appreciate the attributes and purposes of each, how they are alike and different.

THE FOUNDATION SKILLS NETWORK

The foundation skills are those critical cognitive, visual, and fine motor skills that contribute to the development of writing and to the development of handwriting. There are four basic sets of skills that interact to form the foundation skills network for written expression and its necessary supportive areas, for example, handwriting skills, organizing compositions, and including all critical features or components.

One is classification. The ability to classify objects and ideas in the world with one's language is important to both oral and written expression. Activities encouraging children to classify nonprint or nonlinguistic elements such as geometric shapes and symbols of various sorts are especially helpful.

A second set of skills is that of seriation or ordering. The ability to arrange objects, ideas, and events in proper order is central to organizing oral and written language. Children should be presented numerous opportunities to order the various elements in their world. These should include activities where ordering is by size, color, shape, chronology, importance, and aesthetic quality, thus enabling children to deal with very concrete ideas as well as fairly abstract ones.

Spatial relations constitute a third set of skills in the foundation skills network. The ability to place things and ideas in relation to one another as well as in relation to other more extraneous factors is important to writing development.

The final skill set in the group of foundation skills is the fine motor/eye-hand coordination group. Whereas the previous three sets dealt with cognitive matters primarily (and thus contribute most directly to the development of writing-as-conceptual-act), this fourth group of skills is aimed at the necessary facilities for handwriting growth. All, however, contribute to the total writing development of the young child.

USING SYMBOLS

The ability to use symbols is perhaps the most critical of all of the abilities the child must develop to be an effective writer. The child must come to see language use in all of its manifestations as an abstract symbolizing process. And to do this, the child must first come to grips with the character of symbol—what it is, how it can be created, and what its uses are. This can be achieved through four different skill sets: in play, in drawing, in music, and in drama.

Play is perhaps the first area of personal experience where the child, on his own, begins to utilize objects as symbols (for example, the broomstick for the horse, the piece of scrap lumber or a board for a boat). Developmentalists argue that this important role of play helps the child cognitively and provides a critical step on the road to writing development. Physical play is especially appealing to young children. It can be combined with a variety of other skill development categories to assist in the growing understanding of symbol.

Language play begins in the earliest language formation stages of the child. Initially, this is for purposes of learning the sounds and rhythms of the language. As the child grows into the grammar-elaborating stages, after about 24 months, there are many opportunities to turn this language play into useful play for developing a sense of metalinguistic awareness and the potential of language in its inherent symbolic character.

Children, very early in their lives, love to draw. It appears even to be an innate drive that moves children to make graphic representations on paper and other surfaces. Drawing serves multiple purposes. It assists in the development of fine motor skills and eye-hand coordination. It helps the child develop an appreciation for art. And, in writing development, *drawing is the precursor of pictography, the first graphic expression with the symbolic features closest to the ideographs humans employ in writing. Drawing is possibly the most important single activity that assists both writing development and handwriting development. It is critical to the child's evolving sense of symbol, and it directly assists muscle and eye-hand coordination development.*

As with art, music represents an ultimate form of symbolism similar to but different from written language. The similarities, however, are critical and accessible to the young child. Music is symbolic. It is rhythmic. It is holistic. It is sequential. It is cohesive. All of these features can be grasped in rudimentary fashion by the child, and all of these features are important to writing and its development.

Drama is last, but not least, in our framework of skills. Drama is excellent for developing *all* of the other areas we have addressed. The child can explore imaginary worlds, formulate stories, test rhythmic senses, practice muscle coordination, establish symbols and change them around—all without jeopardizing the security of the object world of reality. Nothing in drama is irremediably lost, since drama is a special preserve for make-believe.

Demands on creativity and cognitive abilities range from minimal to optimal. Further, dramatic types can range from interpretive, where the child is provided with all necessary support materials and information, to improvisational, where the child pretends and explores with few directions. Regardless of dramatic type, it is important for the child to have experiences in dramatic activities to assist in an understanding of writing-as-conceptual-act.

A WRITING DEVELOPMENT FRAMEWORK FOR PRESCHOOL/KINDERGARTEN CHILDREN

Table 3–1 presents our framework for developing important writing skills in preschool/kindergarten children. Again, observe that we are categorizing skills and activities so that we can more easily get "handles" on their utilization. However, there is much overlapping. Oral language can be seen as central to all of the skills in the foundation skills network and in the using symbols strand. Creative dramatics can be a setting for getting at any skill in any strand. A child incorporates seriation while elaborating a narrative in either oral language or writing. And we could go on at length pointing out the interrelationships that hold across the three skill strands.

The teacher needs to incorporate and integrate as many of these skills as possible in developing teaching techniques and strategies. The teacher should also remember that an effective writing development program capitalizes upon a variety of learning opportunities within the writing development framework on a fairly regular basis for young children. A checklist such as that shown in Table 3–2 is recommended for the educator to employ in monitoring the program. This checklist, it should be emphasized, is *not* a prescriptive set of activities to be utilized in an ordered fashion but rather simply a part of an overall monitoring system.

For the early childhood educator in a preschool setting, the writing development framework does represent a curriculum design that should lead into school-year programs in language arts in an especially effective fashion. For the parent in a home setting, it represents an excellent opportunity to provide writing development learning experiences that can be extremely valuable and rewarding. For the kindergarten teacher, here is the outline of a comprehensive writing development program with appropriate categories of skills and knowledge for beginning writing instruction.

Materials

This section offers suggestions for materials, supplies, equipment, and settings that are desirable for implementation of the suggested activities and procedures in the framework. Although some of these items or elements are likely to be found only in an early childhood education center of some sort, the author has attempted to identify materials and settings in most cases that can be found in the home or obtained for a home setting at minimum expense.

A few general observations about the recommended materials and equipment are in order.

1. Keep safety in mind as a fundamental rule to be observed. If materials appear to be potentially dangerous (for example, if they have sharp corners or angles, or are "tippy" with unstable balance), avoid them. Writing utensils can be difficult to make totally safe, since there must be some sort of point for marking.

TABLE 3–1. A Writing Development Framework for Preschool/Kindergarten Children

EXPLOITING ORAL LANGUAGE	THE FOUNDATION SKILLS NETWORK	USING SYMBOLS
Using narrative (telling stories)	Classification	In play
Oral → Written	Orally → Geometrically → Symbolically	Physical → Language
Using exposition (describing/explaining)	Seriation Size/color/shape	In drawing
Oral → Written	Chronology Importance Aesthetic quality	Basic Strokes → Picto-graphy → Ideo-graphy
Using persuasion (arguing)	Spatial relations	In music
Oral → Written	Inside → out Outside → in	In drama
	Fine motor (small muscle)/ eye-hand coordination	Interpretive → Improvisational

TABLE 3–2. A Writing Development Activities Checklist

STRANDS	MON.	TUE.	WED.	THURS.	FRI.
I. Oral Language					
A. Telling stories					
B. Describing events					
C. Explaining ideas					
D. Persuading others					
II. Foundation Skills Network					
A. Classification					
Oral					
Geometric shape					
Symbolic					
B. Seriation (ordering)					
Size, shape, color					
Chronology					
Importance					
Aesthetics					
C. Spatial relations					
Inside out					
Outside in					
D. Fine motor/eye-hand					
coordination					
III. Using Symbols					
A. Play					
B. Drawing					
Basic strokes					
Pictography					
Ideography					
C. Drama					
Interpretive					
Improvisational					

✔ for each day of the week where activities took place; multiple ✔ for skill categories where one activity incorporates others to a major extent.

Common-sense knowledge about materials and sensitivity to the child's maturity should provide reasonable guidance.

2. Carefully assess the child's physical development before procuring materials or designing special learning settings. Children develop considerably in all areas between the ages of 3 and 6, for example, and what might be suitable for one child may be useless to another. Since there is considerable variation in development within the same age range, even age-matched children must be considered on an individual basis.

Generally speaking, the following characteristics of physical abilities may be assumed for most children in the assigned age group. Remember, however, that these characteristics are quite general and, even so, just estimates for most children:

Age, 3 to 4 years	*Age, 5 to 6 years*
jump or hop on one foot	run, jump, climb or skip with good coordination
climb stair using alternate feet	
walk on a balance beam	jump rope and walk a balance beam with ease
ride a tricycle	
stand on one foot for a brief period	ride a two-wheel bike
	tie shoes, dress self, coordinate body movements to the rhythm of music

3. The materials and equipment included in this section will not be comprehensive in the sense of being aimed at total child development. We are concerned with developing *writing* abilities.

4. The materials and equipment included here are intended to be neither exhaustive nor necessary in their entirety. Hopefully, many instructional settings will have a greater array and variety of these things. On the other hand, everything included here is not necessary in assisting the child in developing writing abilities. What are included are intended to serve as examples and are suggestive rather than prescriptive.

Building materials   Fine motor skills and eye-hand coordination are critical to writing development. Therefore, any objects or materials that help the child develop these skills are useful. Included are:

building blocks, either commercially produced or homemade

small accessory play items—toy trucks, cars, trains, furniture, wooden or plastic figures and animals, barns, etc.

work benches with peg boards, mallets and other building tools and supplies

clay, dominoes, inlays, puzzles

snap-lock beads, wooden beads, stacking rings

wooden lumber scraps, wooden dowels, empty thread spools, small wooden or plastic containers, cardboard cylinders

sand and sandbox

Art and writing supplies   Like building materials, art and writing supplies are helpful in developing fine motor skills and eye-hand coordination as well as useful for actual writing and drawing. Included are:

crayons of various sizes and colors

pencils of various sizes

felt-tip markers of various sizes and colors

paper, both lined and unlined

glue and paste

blunt-nosed scissors

brushes and paints (liquid tempera and fingerpaint)

yarn, string, pipestem cleaners, and glitter

coloring books and tracing books

templates (plastic, wood, or heavy cardboard) or geometric shapes, basic strokes and letters of the alphabet—both manuscript and cursive and letters in both capital and lowercase form. Templates may be purchased commercially (they are included in many published handwriting programs) at office supply vendors. They may also be made. If made, remember to develop initial sets with straight single lines, angles, and circles.

Music supplies and equipment   Music is important for developing not only physical coordination but also sense of rhythm, linearity, and cohesion in a composition. Music supplies and equipment include:

piano and/or guitar

autoharp, records, song flute, tone blocks, bells

record player and records

tape recorder (preferably cassette type)

Dramatic play materials   Drama is one of the areas where the child can utilize *all* skills critical to writing development as well as the other language skills. Dramatic play materials include

both large puppets and finger puppets (finger puppets are easily made)

multicultural dolls and related clothes, furniture, and accessories appropriate to each

costumes and masks (old clothing, shoes, and hats make excellent improvisational "stage" costumes)

large free-standing cardboard or plywood backdrops for some of the more serious productions

Language development materials and equipment   Language development will obviously be a major beneficiary of all the supplies-and-materials categories. However, to emphasize this area the following need be considered:

books—picture, alphabet, and story books

tape recorder (cassette) and a number of tapes

record player and records

Exploration and problem-solving materials   In addition to the supplies and equipment already listed, some exploration and problem-solving materials that could be included are:

small collections—rocks, insects, or shells

terrariums and aquariums

stethoscope

magnifying glass

tuning forks, magnets, nuts and bolts

maps

rain gauges, weathervanes, and other devices for measuring the weather
prisms
small shovels, pails, and cups
cookie cutters

In addition to this array of materials and supplies, the educator needs to consider the possibility of learning centers where each of these categories of materials might provide focused learning opportunities. Specifically, it is desirable to set up a special writing center with table, chairs, paper, writing utensils, and books where the child may go to produce written expression. The learning center concept places a premium on particular learning experiences and establishes a minienvironment that encourages productive learning for the child. If aides or volunteers are available in an early-education setting, it is relatively easy to set up job responsibilities and then establish a monitoring routine for the head teacher or center administrator to use. The learning center concept also lends itself well to a variety of educational philosophies, ranging from totally free and unstructured to more formally structured programs.

Most parents in the home can even find accessible space to establish a limited number of small learning centers. An art and writing center could serve a double function for the young child.

Regardless of whether learning centers are established, there are a number of characteristics central to an effective learning environment and of which teachers of young children must be aware.

A Sincere Attitude.   Boys and girls from 3 to 6 are developing human beings, naive about some things but sophisticated about some others. The teacher should always reflect a sincere attitude in teaching children.

A Respectful Attitude.   The educator of young children must have respect for the child, for self, and for the language. Language is the foundation and, more, the building material of written expression. Respect for its potential must be reflected.

An Open and Flexible Approach.   Research indicates that with the young child more productive and higher quality expression occurs where the child has freedom of movement, self-choice, a variety of options, and freedom to change direction of learning and play pursuits as desired.

An Imaginative Environment.   Children are like adults in that their patience in a given setting is directly related to their interest in its content. Striving for creative materials, activities, and purposes is paramount.

EXPLOITING ORAL LANGUAGE

Using Narrative (Telling Stories)

As you will recall from our examination of the research, children as young as 2 years of age have a sense of story structure and its important elements such as character, plot, setting, and conflict. We want to make sure that they have every opportunity to capitalize upon the oral traditions of language and literature to further develop the components of story structure, for this knowledge and these language skills are critical to writing. The earliest efforts to write typically focus upon stories, and the more graphic and extensive the story structure knowledge the child brings to the task, the more likely successful early writing experience will be. In addition, the ability to tell and write effective stories encompasses a variety of skills necessary for other writing tasks; therefore, transfer potential is very strong here.

Child readiness　　It is, indeed, rare to find the child not ready to listen to a story, so the following suggested inventory is primarily aimed at story production readiness in the child.

STORYTELLING READINESS INVENTORY

	YES	NO
1. The child listens attentively as you read a story.	____	____
2. The child listens attentively as you tell a story.	____	____
3. The child enjoys looking through picture books alone.	____	____
4. The child enjoys talking about the content of books.	____	____
5. Given a cue such as a picture or model, the child can make up a short story.	____	____
6. The child can be observed in play situations to make up scenes, skits, or stories to act out.	____	____
7. The child can be observed telling stories to peers.	____	____
8. The child often listens to poetry or prose on records or the radio and enjoys discussing it with others.	____	____
9. The child enjoys talking about the content of television seen or books or stories read.	____	____

The above inventory should be used as a general guide to readiness, with adjustments made accordingly in the selection of activities and materials for use.

Listening to stories　　Reading and telling stories to adults as well as children is an historical tradition. And it is indeed rare to find the child who does not enjoy being read to. *Children should have stories read to them daily.* The stories need not be long or overly detailed for the young child, but regularity of the performance is important.

During the reading it is helpful to pause at appropriate places to encourage commentary and observations from the child. Focus on a picture or art work in the book and ask the child about its content or raise questions that tie it to important facets of the story you are reading. Pause during the reading of the narrative to ask the child to comment on the narrative. Questions suggestive of incidents in the story are excellent: "Why do you think he did _____?" or "How do you suppose she was able to _____?" or "What would you have done if you were _____?"

Questions that encourage the child to assume empathetic roles with characters or to guess at later developments in the story line are helpful.

For storytelling purposes, picture books are excellent challenges to both the reader and the listener. They offer an excellent opportunity to develop imagination and a chance to elaborate story plots. Adults should read enough stories from actual narrative as well as tell stories by using a picture book to provide the basis of the story grammar. Procedurally, however, one should use the same general approach in both picture and print narratives. Allow the child to interject comment, and frequently pause and probe with questions. Be alert to waning interest, and do not force the child to remain involved when interest suddenly evaporates. Move to some unrelated activity. In selecting materials, look for quality art work and prints as well as interesting and developmentally appropriate stories. Some suggested books are cited below.

PICTURE BOOKS

ANNO, M. *Anno's Italy*. Cleveland: Collins World, 1980.
ARDIZZONE, E. *The Wrong Side of the Bed*. Garden City: Doubleday, 1970.
CARLE, E. *I See a Song*. New York: Crowell, 1973.
FUCHS, E. *Journey to the Moon*. New York: Delacorte, 1964.
GOODALL, J. S. *Naughty Nancy*. New York: Atheneum, 1975.
HOGROGRIAN, N. *Apples*. New York: MacMillan, 1972.
KENT, J. *The Egg Book*. New York: Macmillan, 1975.
KRAHN, F. *Who's Seen the Scissors?* New York: E. P. Dutton, 1975.
MAYER, M. *Ah-Choo*. New York: Dial Press, 1976.
_____. *A Boy, A Dog and a Frog*. New York: Dial Press, 1967.
SCHWENINGER, A. *A Dance For Three*. New York: Dial Press, 1979.
TURKEL, B. *Deep in the Forest*. New York: E. P. Dutton, 1976.
WEZEL, P. *The Good Bird*. New York: Harper & Row, 1964.
WINTER, P. *The Bear and the Fly*. New York: Crown, 1976.

BOOKS FOR STORYTELLING

BAILEY, C. S. *The Little Rabbit Who Wanted Red Wings*. New York: Platt and Munk, 1945.
BROWN, M. *Stone Soup*. New York: Scribner's, 1947.
DOMANSKA, J. *The Turnip*. New York: Macmillan, 1969.
GALDONE, P. *The Gingerbread Boy*. New York: Seabury, 1975.
_____. *The Three Bears*. New York: Seabury, 1972.
GINSBURG, M. *Mushroom in the Rain*. New York: Macmillan, 1974.
HOGROGRIAN, N. *Carrot Cake*. New York: Greenwillow, 1977.
_____. *One Fine Day*. New York: Macmillan, 1971.
KENT, J. *The Fat Cat*. New York: Parents Magazine Press, 1971.
KRASILOUSKY, P. *The Man Who Didn't Wash His Dishes*. New York: Doubleday, 1950.
KRAUSS, R. *The Carrot Seed*. New York: Harper, 1945.

LIPKIND, W., and MORDINIVOFF, N.   *Finders Keepers.* New York: Harcourt Brace Jovanovich, 1951.
LABEL, A.   *How the Rooster Saved the Day.* New York: Greenwillow, 1977.
MILES, M.   *Chicken Forgets.* Boston: Little, Brown, 1976.
MOSEL, A.   *Tikki Tikki Tembo.* New York: Holt, Rinehart & Winston, 1968.
PRESTON, E.   *One Dark Night.* New York: The Viking Press, 1969.
TRESSELT, A.   *The Mitten.* New York: Lothrop, 1964.
WILDSMITH, B.   *Python's Party.* New York: Franklin Watts, 1975.
WILLIAMS, J.   *One Big Wish.* New York: Macmillan, 1980.

Telling stories   When the child appears to show enough interest and maturity, he or she would be encouraged to elaborate on stories. Initially, the young child should not be expected to detail a complete story from scratch, that is, without book, photos, models, or cues. In fact, initial activities ought to focus upon "story completer" activities such as the following.

Picture sequencing   The child is given a set of several pictures or photos that, when arranged in sequence, suggest an event or short story. The child then rearranges them from the scrambled order and tells why he or she chose the order selected. The child might then construct a story orally from the picture sequence.

Pictures such as these are available from a variety of commerical publishers and can also be cut out of old books, magazines, or newspapers. In addition, the pictures can be drawn on cardboard squares and then cut apart.

Making up missing parts   Another lead into complete story-telling is that where the teacher or parent creates a simple story, tells it up to a critical point, and then asks the child to finish. For example, "Once upon a time a little bear got into lots of trouble. His mother told him to go to his room and take a nap. He sneaked out a window in his room and ran into the woods to play instead. He didn't pay attention and it was soon dark. He forgot how to get back home so he . . . [ask child to finish]." The child is thus provided nearly all of the story and is to produce only the ending. Of course, the amount of information provided to the child can be reduced or added to. Further, the complexity of the story plot can be easily controlled as well, all to accommodate the child's state of readiness.

Scribble writing stories   Once children are fairly comfortable with the process of telling stories orally, they should be encouraged to write stories. They may resist initially, feeling that they do not know how to write. Encourage them to use paper and pencil to produce marks while you create a story in writing yourself. Then each will "read" his or her story to the other. The adult in this case should actually compose a story.

Activities such as this play two critical roles. First, they indicate the personal value the educator and the parent place upon writing. And, second, they constitute an initial step for the child in coming to see writing as a communicating tool. Remember, however, that in the early stages the child is not likely to make a serious connection between the story produced and the marks made on the paper. He or she is simply imitating an adult process as seen and is not likely to connect what is said to the paper, that is, to see the marks as mnemonic characters. Therefore, do not expect the child to pick up the paper a few minutes later and "read" the same story back to you that was created moments before. Over a period of time, with implementation of the complete framework of writing development skills, however, the child will conceptualize the writing process effectively.

Using Exposition

Expository skills normally develop in concert with the ability to develop narrative. Exposition, however, is somewhat less personal and more objective in character. In the very young, therefore, it will be more difficult to master. The following readiness inventory can be helpful:

DESCRIBING/EXPLAINING ABILITY READINESS INVENTORY

	YES	NO
1. The child can follow a simple set of directions.	_____	_____
2. The child can describe a favorite personal belonging with reasonable accuracy.	_____	_____
3. The child can identify a number of important people in his or her life.	_____	_____
4. The child can tell how to do a simple task, such as assemble a simple toy or object.	_____	_____
5. The child can tell why a simple step was taken or why an action was taken, for example, two animals fighting over food.	_____	_____

The child who can handle most of the tasks identified in this readiness inventory is prepared to produce the language of exposition (describing/explaining).

It is well to remember that, for most of us, this mode of written expression will be the one we use more than any other in our lives. Even letters, diaries, reports, and directions to friends often derive from this mode. For the young child, this mode is the formative oral language, the one that generates most other language growth. The following activities and ideas should assist in this development as well as that of written expression.

Questioning   "What" and "where" questions help elicit talk to describe or inform:

What does that toy look like?
Where are grandfather's cows?

"Why" and "how" questions help elicit talk to explain or justify a belief:

> Why is the dog running away?
> How does this toy work?

Statements "I think" statements encourage elaboration of description or informing talk:

> I think we should have gone on a picnic, don't you?
> I think you're just teasing me!

"I'll bet you can't" challenges call for friendly descriptive responses:

> I'll bet you can't tie that shoe!
> I'll bet you can't tell me what the story was about!

Show-and-tell Show-and-tell activities have traditionally been successful with children. In its simplest form, show-and-tell is an activity in which children bring before a group of their peers an object or item of interest that they then describe.

Initially, the early childhood educator may need to provide considerable incentive, encouragement, and probing questions that will assist the child in describing his or her show-and-tell object to others. However, before long, the young child will feel confident and excited about the activity.

Show-and-tell presentations ought to be of a variety that encourages both describing and explaining language. If children bring only items that they describe, one can introduce explanatory language by means of "why" questions. In fact, a useful point to remember is that any response to a "why" question must be couched in the explanatory mode even if the child is not aware of it. Do remember, however, that the difference between the language of description and explanation is very subtle. And, developmentally, children cannot make the technical distinction until they are into the intermediate grades. However, we need to provide language-using environments early on that help children develop a sense of language use for different purposes.

Telling about "Telling about" is an easier format than show-and-tell in that it can be more readily created in a home setting. Only the child and one other person are needed. It is more demanding in that the child must deal more abstractly with language, since there is not a physical object present to describe. The child must rely on the language rather than the physical presence for the describing/explaining. The educator or parent must be prepared to assist with guidance and appropriate questions and be a supportive, interested audience.

Some possibilities:

tell about your trip to Grandma's
tell about your trip to the farm

or,

tell about the time your dog was sick
tell about the time you were lost

or,

tell about what you would like for your birthday
tell why you like parties
tell why you like trips

Using Persuasion

Argumentation or persuasion is a demanding mode of presentation. Research with older children indicates that it requires and facilitates the most complex sentence structures the user is likely to employ. However, we know that young children use argumentation regularly in their oral language. They do not have the sophistication of older children in this area, but they understand and employ persuasion effectively in fundamental ways.

Following is a readiness inventory to be used for this language mode:

PERSUADING ABILITY READINESS INVENTORY

	YES	NO
1. The child is not intimidated by controversy.	_____	_____
2. The child enjoys give and take.	_____	_____
3. The child can present a persuasive argument for something, for example, why he or she should not have to go to bed right now.	_____	_____
4. The child has a positive self concept.	_____	_____
5. The child is acceptive when he or she doesn't get a desired object or preference.	_____	_____
6. The child shows "grit", that is, is willing to stand up for what he or she believes.	_____	_____
7. The child enjoys playful banter.	_____	_____

Persuasion is possibly the most elegant and demanding of writing uses. Some suggested persuasion language use activities follow.

Providing alternatives   Look for opportunities where you can give the child options, and ask the child to tell why he or she should be permitted the option chosen or to explain why the alternative was selected. For example:

You may play indoors or ourdoors during free time. Which do you want to do? Why?
Choose between two books for storytelling time.
We're going to make cookies. Which kind do you want (provide two choices)?

Problem solving in the group   Show children large pictures with telling scenes, for example, a picture of a small boy about to step from a curb in front of a moving bus while a small girl runs toward him attempting to warn him of the danger. Then encourage them to explore for cause-effect connections or project what is about to happen. Encourage them to look first at the whole. In the above situations, a question such as "What is happening in this picture?" is better than "What is in this picture?" (The latter implicitly encourages labeling rather than elaboration.)

Here are a few suggestions about oral language use generally that the educator and parent should keep in mind:

> Include the child in conversation at dinner, during TV watching, during chore time, that is, during all normal conversation periods and not just at times of discipline or when the child is being given a directive.
>
> Don't underestimate a child's language ability. Research has shown that children tend to use more complex language with other children than they do with adults.
>
> Compliment and encourage rather than criticize or correct. Research has shown that correction of the young child's grammar by adults tends *not* to have positive effect.
>
> The growing child uses language for learning as well as for communication purposes. Prior to 7 years of age or so, there is a great deal of egocentric or self-centered talk in the child's language use.
>
> Encourage the child to elaborate with language. Begin descriptions and explanations with overview statements that are followed with statements describing what makes up the overview. Try not to encourage "labeling," but instead encourage the child to move from the general to the more specific. Encourage the child to select specific and helpful descriptions that are telling, for example, adjectives or describing terms that help to identify or explain the thing or person being talked or written about.

THE FOUNDATION SKILLS NETWORK

The three foundation skill areas—classification, seriation, and spatial relations—represent skills that range from relatively simple to extremely complex. Their place in the writing development framework is logically fixed. They represent key opportunities to relate thinking to written expression and, further, add a strong dimension of variety at key places in an early writing program.

A readiness inventory that will be of assistance to the educator in determining the child's readiness in these first three parts of the foundation skills network follows.

A READINESS INVENTORY FOR THE FOUNDATION SKILLS NETWORK

	YES	NO
1. Does the child display "object permanence"—that is, exhibit behavior indicating that he or she knows that movement of an object simply relocates the same object? (One cue is that eyes will follow your movement of the object.)	_____	_____
2. Can the child indicate which of two objects is larger where the size difference is significant?	_____	_____
3. Can the child tell you how three figures—a cardboard square colored red, a cardboard circle colored yellow, and a blue triangle of cardboard—are alike and how they are different by identifying important distinguishing features?	_____	_____
4. Can the child order three different sized objects (for example, buttons, chips, and beads) from largest to smallest?	_____	_____
5. When playing with toys, does the child attempt to cluster or group things in reasonably logical places (for examples, with a toy farm place the animals and barn away from the house somewhat)?	_____	_____
6. Does the child make some effort to choose toys that are reasonably proportioned in relation to one another when such are available?	_____	_____

If the child has difficulties with the above, it is wise to consider activities of the very simplest sort modeled after those that follow in each of the areas of classification, seriation, and spatial relations.

Classification

The ability to classify objects, events, and people—and to classify language with language—is fundamental to both reading and writing development in the child. However, there are a few things that must be kept in mind when undertaking such activities. Children prior to 7 years of age lack certain cognitive abilities. For example, given several red beads and several blue beads and asked to put them in two different piles, the color cue is likely to be enough to lead to success by many children. However, the task depicted in Figure 3–1 would be far more difficult. Given:

Question: Are there more red things or more triangles?

Classification tasks where more than one property or factor has to be kept in mind can confuse a child in this stage of cognitive development. Tasks initially should be quite simple and designed to generate interest and language as much as success in the task itself. Begin with simple classification of nonprint objects, for example, cardboard cutouts of geometric shapes, wooden or plastic figures, simple pictures. Then move to more demanding tasks. The following should serve as sample activities.

Figure 3–1.

Geometric Shapes

1. Materials—cardboard cutouts or squares, circles, and triangles, all the same color and size.
   Task—place them into three like groups.
   Discussion—ask the child why he or she chose the items picked.
2. Materials—the same as in 1 but half of each—squares, circles, triangles—colored red, the other half blue.
   Task—place them into three like groups.
   Discussion—ask the child to explain his or her choices.
3. Do the same as in 2, but ask for two groups instead of three (color then becomes the critical factor).

Flannel board creatures   Prepare a flannel board by outlining a lake or pond with trees on the shore and a marshy edge or shoreline with a couple of logs or rocks on the edge of the water. Trim our several animals, for example, a fish, a bird, a frog, a rabbit, a deer. Then have the child place the animals in appropriate places. Encourage discussion afterward with "why" questions.

Sandbox environments   Have the child use miniature plastic figures to build a farm in a sandbox environment. Discuss where the animals should go, where people should be, and so on.

Story types   Tell the child you are going to read or tell two different stories. Choose two brief selections, one fiction with clear story grammar cues (for example, a "Once upon a time" beginning) and one nonfiction. After presenting them, ask which was "make believe" and which was "real." Talk about the differences.

Scribble writing and different writing forms   Ask the child to write a letter to a friend telling her what she recently did on a trip or other fun activity. A bit later ask the child to make up a story about a recent event or incident that was interesting or important to the child. Remember to sit with the child and write your own version in each case. Take turns "reading" your letters and your stories, and discuss them with each other.

Seriation

The ability to place things, events, and ideas in proper order is very important to writing. Yet, according to a recent assessment of writing abilities nationwide in 9-, 13-, and 17-year-olds, the ability to sequence ideas so they follow reasonably and logically from one another remains a serious problem in children's writing. Having a variety of experiences in this area is important for the young child's later success as a writer.

Object seriation   Activities in seriation should begin with the simple task of ordering two or three objects such as geometric shapes, chips, buttons, or beads according to size. As the child becomes more proficient, complexity can be increased by increasing the number or types of objects being ordered and by reducing the difference in the size of objects the child is working with.

One interesting thing the educator will note is that children can draw a series of rods ranging in height from short to long at an earlier age than they can actually seriate the objects themselves. Notice that drawing does not demand reversibility capacity in the child, that is, the child does not need to be thinking constantly about a given rod in relation to all others. The drawing fixes position on the paper and freezes the relationship to all those that come before. This is perhaps an instance where cognition outstrips fine motor skill, though not by much. Drawing a rod is essentially drawing a straight vertical line, which is one of the basic strokes for prehandwriting instruction.

This, in fact, is an excellent opportunity for integrating skills in the foundation skills network. The educator can make cutout cardboard squares with one of the nine basic strokes on five or six squares in successively smaller sizes. Design sets for each of the basic strokes. Then design multiple sets where the cardboard squares are the same size but the basic stroke varies in size, as in Figure 3–2.

In a later step the stroke cards can be scrambled so that each of the nine basic strokes is mixed in with others. Children can then order the squares by comparing the size of one basic stroke to the others provided. At still a later stage, blank cardboard squares can be provided, and the children can form basic strokes in descending or ascending size. Obviously, this could also be done on paper. However, the child's cardboard cutouts can be used in later scrambling activities also.

Another example of skill development integration in our writing development framework is in the area of drawing and seriation. Learning to draw pictures of events or scenes involving people, animals, and objects requires a developing skill at depicting things in such a manner as to suggest proportion and relative size. A more complicated and later-developing facility is that of using relative size to reflect depth and space in a drawing. (Notice the dual factors here, which partially explain the later development of depth-depicting ability.) Suggested activities will be included in a later section on drawing.

Seriation of picture stories   Since story writing constitutes a major portion of the early writing of children, it is particularly important that young children have a variety of involvements with stories—having stories read to them, making up their own, and acting out stories in dramatic settings. Within the foundation skills network, seriation represents an excellent place to begin initial work in the formalization of children's experience with the order and logic of story elements.

Figure 3-2. The Stroke Cards.

Initially the teacher might present the child with four or five pictures or photos that have temporal or chronological relation to one another. For example, sequential family photos or pictures cut out of old picture books are excellent. The creative artist could draw pictures on paper or cardboard, enabling the teacher or parent to personalize the activity by using pictures of people, animals, or activities the child knows.

Remember that there are numerous variations of this activity other than giving the pictures to the child and asking the child to order them. One can sequence and place a card or two out of order and ask the child to correct them. If the child possesses advanced drawing skills, he or she can draw a picture that could logically follow from the others. Notice the excellent opportunities to incorporate oral language to encourage the child to articulate ideas as the child physically works through the task of ordering the pictures. Why did you put this one here? Is there any other way they can go? How would it change things if we moved this one to this place over here? Can you tell me a story that is happening here?

Another activity is to cluster pictures into groups of two or three. (Tape them together if photos. If you are drawing the pictures yourself, draw two or three in sequence before you cut them apart.) Then ask the child to order these strips of pictures in proper sequence. The child thus learns to look at larger chunks of meaning for story building and has the opportunity to begin to see how larger units of meaning fit together in a cohesive fashion.

Writing captions for picture stories   Picture stories may be captioned in two ways. One can write appropriate story lines under the pictures or picture clusters, or draw empty ''word balloons'' over the characters, as is done in comic books and newspaper cartoon strips. Children can be encouraged to make up story lines to correspond to the incidents in the pictures. Remember that the word balloons need to be large enough to accommodate fine motor skills that are not particularly refined. If the child balks at engaging in activities such as this initially, the activities should be postponed until the child appears ready to participate. It is important, however, that the child be given maximal opportunity to relate written expression to story structure.

Using ordered dictation and mnemonics for early writing   Learning to associate marks made on paper with ideas given orally emphasizes the mnemonic and symbolic potential of the marks.

Tell the child that you are going to say some things and that he or she should use the pencil and paper in whatever ways are helpful to recall the ideas. Then say the following in order:

1. a little duck
2. a little duck sitting by the pond
3. a lot of little ducks are sitting by a pond on the big farm

Encourage the child to use marks to remember what was said. Check to see whether the child attempts to adjust the length of marks to correspond to the length of the utterances. Remember to keep the quantity of utterances small (perhaps only three or four), the ideas relatively simple, and the events described within the experience range of the child.

Another approach is to order the utterances by length. This is best done practicing short to long progressions.

Seriation by quality   Ordering by importance or by aesthetic qualities, though more abstract, is also easier than other seriation activities in some senses. The teacher might ask the child to place a series of photos in sequence from those liked best to those liked least, for example.

One of the major features of seriation by quality is the opportunity to utilize oral language generally and the language of description specifically. ''Why'' questions can be employed effectively by the teacher or parent, implicitly leading the child away from general pronouns so often employed to specific adjectives and adverbs that identify more precisely the characteristics of the things involved.

In addition to the aesthetic sequencing of pictures or photos, other possibilities include food, toys, games, and collections (of rocks, shells, or stamps). Also, the variations suggested for seriation activities earlier are possible in this category as well.

Spatial Relations

Writing requires an ability to project space, line length, and total volume required for a given written message. It requires that the producer of the writing have some overall image of the graphic look of the writing after it is completed. Clearly, spatial relations activities are called for in the experience of the young child.

The child needs practice in spatial relations exercises that require him or her to see other things, people, and events from the personal or ''I'' point of view (inside-out), that is, how do things look to you from where you are right now? In addition, the child has to learn to look at things from another person's point of view (outside-in), for example, as if one were located elsewhere or were in someone else's shoes, so to speak. This latter ability, or (as it is sometimes called) the ability to psychologically distance oneself from the immediate actual situation, is critical to more effective writing skills necessary for the child during the school years. The ability to establish a psychological distance, however, is a very demanding cognitive skill.

Preschoolers cannot be expected to reflect a great deal of skill in this area in its more sophisticated aspects. However, initial activities in spatial relations can serve an important role in providing basic experiences that can help the child in developing these abilities.

Orientation activities

Give the child a sheet of paper divided into four squares, for example:

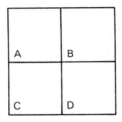

In the upper lefthand corner of each square, place an easily identifiable shape, draw-

ing, or picture, for example, a drawing of the sun, that is, ☀ in box A, a star in

B, etc. Then ask the child to put a mark in the appropriate square as you give the identifying sign, For example, "Put an X in the square with the star."

Do this with a variety of geometric shapes. For example, use circles and triangles, dividing them into subunits and employing the same approach. Increase difficulty by increasing the number of compartments in the geometric shape and by altering the sophistication of the verbal cues.

This particular activity works well with the framework strand on "Using Symbols, Drawing (see Table 3–1, p. 42)." For example, activities can move from those with

realistic picture cues, for example, sun and stars, to pictographs where 👤 can

represent "boy," to the word *boy*. This movement toward the use of actual words serving as cues should be gradual and should coincide with other activities that are leading the child toward a recognition and utilization of symbols.

Use a variety of pictures or photographs of the same object and ask the child to tell whether it's a "bird's-eye view" or a "worm's-eye view," as for example, in a picture of a table from a ground-level perspective as opposed to a view of the table from above.

Present pictures or photographs to the child that contain objects or people in closeup as well as farther away in relation to each other and the camera. Ask the child to indicate which elements are the closest and which are the farthest away.

Inside-out and outside-in spatial relations activities   The purpose of these

activities is to help the child extend point of view from self to others.

Place a toy barn or other building in the center of a sandbox and encourage or participate with the child in building outward from the barn to design a farm with animals, toy trucks, and tractors.

In other settings use small sticks or small stones to outline an area in the sandbox. Suggest that this is a fence enclosing a farm. Encourage the child to then use toy figures and buildings to design a farm within the boundaries of the fence.

Use tinker toys to form a small square with ample empty slots at each corner. Encourage the child to create a larger construction by adding to the starter square, thus building outward.

Alternatively, form a large square with tinker toys and suggest the child work within to extend the construction inward. (In early stages this will require adult assistance.)

Connecting the dots   Either use commercially published connect-the-dot books or design materials of your own. Provide the child with a variety of dot-connecting projects at appropriate levels of complexity. Be sure there are some activities where the child begins within the figure to be produced and works outward connecting the dots and others where the child starts on the perimeter of the figure and works inward. Keep in mind the nine basic strokes of handwriting, and look to the selection of activities that are interesting to the child, appropriate in complexity level, and that incorporate the fundamental character of the basic handwriting strokes.

Fine Motor (Small Muscle)/Eye-Hand Coordination

This is the skill development area within the foundation skills network that many feel is one of the most critical of all for writing development.

In determining child readiness for this last skill area in the foundation skills network, the teacher needs to observe carefully how well the child can handle the less sophisticated building and assembling tasks before going into the more complex activities.

In addition to this general ongoing monitoring, the following readiness inventory can serve as a useful guide in designing activities:

A FINE MOTOR/EYE-HAND COORDINATION READINESS FOR WRITING INVENTORY

	YES	NO
1. The child can stack a set of different-sized wooden blocks (four or five per set) in a tower.	____	____
2. The child can manipulate fairly small toys deftly, for example, the stethoscope, thermometer, and syringe in a toy doctor's kit.	____	____
3. The child can duplicate a simple geometric construction an adult assembles out of contruction materials such as plastic or wooden blocks, tinker toys, or sticks.	____	____
4. The child can correctly assemble a simple puzzle (three or four large wooden or plastic pieces of simple straight edges or angles).	____	____
5. The child can draw pictures of simple figures or objects that reflect the nine basic strokes of handwriting.	____	____

6. The child can adequately grip a writing utensil of some type—chalk, crayon, pencil, or pen—and control it adequately to make sustained marks in a relatively straight line.   _____ _____

7. The child shows a strong interest in drawing or pretend writing.   _____ _____

8. The child's attention span is of sufficient length to engage in writing-type activities (5 to 10 minutes minimum).   _____ _____

Building activities   Provide the child with ample building materials of various sizes, textures, and shapes. Especially desirable are those that require the child to think about how they can be fitted together, for example, puzzles, building logs, and plastic linking blocks. Variety and easy access for daily involvement are important.

Puppet making and use   Old socks make excellent hand puppets. Painted-on faces or sewn-on eyes, nose, mouth, and ears are relatively easy to fashion. Finger puppets can be made from old cotton gloves, and appropriate characters are easy to create. Children should be encouraged to make up stories about characters and act out their stories with the hand and finger puppets.

Cutting and pasting   Using scissors and paste to create new designs, pictures, or scenes is valuable for the child as an assist to organizing and conceptualizing knowledge as well as developing fine motor skills.

Effective use of scissors with reasonable precision is not likely until about the fourth year. Therefore, parents and educators should take care with 3-year-olds and younger children. Simply giving them old catalogs or magazines with scissors and encouragement to cut can be frustrating. Initial activities should employ precut materials, suitably sized paste brushes, and stable thin cardboard or heavy unlined paper for the child to paste the cutouts on. Gummed backing and a damp sponge rather than paste is ideal but can become somewhat expensive. Old Christmas cards, birthday cards, and other greeting cards with simple designs or subjects with minimum intricate maneuvering required for the scissors make excellent early cutouts. Alternatively, shapes and figures drawn on thin cardboard sheets of small dimensions are also very good.

Adults should demonstrate how a glued-on or stapled support at the base of cutout cardboard figures can enable such figures to stand erect.

Threading and pattern following   Learning how to thread or stitch helps the child learn how to lace and tie shoes. However, such activities are also valuable as assists to fine motor skill development. Early activities for the young can be found in various commercially developed toys utilizing wooden rings or spools of various sizes to be threaded over wooden dowels, for example,

In addition, and for later variety and more complexity, lacing boards can be easily made with a jigsaw, hand drill, small thin plywood board and small pegs, for example,

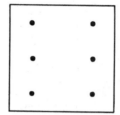

(view from above)

One end of a cord can be tied around one of the pegs in the board, the other end should be tied to a plastic ring for easy control by small fingers. The child can then create a variety of patterns by looping the string around pegs and lacing between them. More pegs can increase the complexity of designs created or to be duplicated by the child if there is a matching board from which to copy.

USING SYMBOLS

The ability to utilize symbols is critical to the development of writing. An individual can get by in the world with minimal handwriting skills. However, no person can compose who does not have a basic grasp of the nature and function of symbols in our society. The more sophisticated one's understanding of symbols and their use, the more likely is one to be a proficient writer. By examining the research literature presented earlier, we can see that a good deal of symbolic awareness develops naturally in the more common language using environments we are in daily. However, that same research suggests that the child's potential in this area is far greater than we give credit for and that encourgement in the development of this potential will produce children who write more effectively and earlier in their lives.

Symbols and Symbolizing in Play

Play might be the single most important part of the early development of cognition in the child, for it is through play that the child first discovers the character of symbols, and, furthermore, it is the first activity in which the child makes serious intentional use of symbols.

Physical play Physical movement play is of essentially two types, productive and reproductive. The first is that which is most common in the earliest years up through the second or third year. Children engage in activities designed to produce an object, events, or relationships. In this stage there are seldom play events or movements that are intended to evoke symbols or even suggest symbolic behavior. The movement of this play is largely done for nonintentional end results.

Reproductive play, however, emerges during the third or fourth year and has as its forms behavior that reconstructs and reproduces realities the child has experienced. In this sense, many movements, objects, and events reflect symbolic potential, although, especially in the earliest stages, this potential often goes unexploited and probably unrecognized.

Playing house, school, cowboys, grocer, and other role-simulation types all fall within this category of play. The broomstick becomes the horse, the lollypop the doctor's thermometer, a piece of wood a truck, and so on.

Of most significance, perhaps, is the fact that the adult need do nothing other than provide space and time for physical movement play to occur. The selection, placement, and timing of objects or toys, however, can be extremely helpful in encouraging the child to engage in reproductive play. A few suggestions that can be useful:

> Carefully choose toys for purchase. Be sure they are age-appropriate, but also select those which are likely to encourage a range of role playing and simulation activities, for it is in these ways that perception and use of symbol evolve.
>
> Consider purchasing toys at times other than special occasions such as birthdays. Observe the child's interests. A small inexpensive purchase at the right time when interest in a topic or idea is high can be especially effective.
>
> Choose toys or objects that are not exact replicas of the real. Choose a toy *selectively* and with taste for its aesthetic and abstract qualities. But, choose that which provides some challenge for the child's imagination and sense of creativity.
>
> If you are a woodworking hobbyist or artist, create for the child. Toy cars, trucks, boats, trains, and planes can be made from scrap wood, jigsaw, sandpaper, and glue.
>
> Play with the child. Be willing to assume symbolic roles and use objects symbolically. The child becomes a special person on such occasions by virtue of your involvement, and the role of symbol as medium of exchange between each other becomes enhanced.

Language play All play encourages language use and is, therefore, important to language development in the child. There is, however, a special delight the child takes in "playing with language," using language not to communicate specific information so much as to make language itself as an object of enjoyment. Using language to talk about language is known technically as *metalanguage*. Adults, as well as children, delight in metalanguage. Puns are the most conspicuous examples of language play by adults, although research now shows that children at early ages (kindergarten and before) can also appreciate them.

Language play is especially helpful in the development of symbol conceptualization by the child, since it focuses not upon what is identified in the object world but instead upon the symbol itself. Much of this language play develops innocently enough for the young child as a function of normal language development. For the very young, practicing the various sounds possible for humans to produce is necessary before the environment indicates to the child which sounds are important to his language. Only a few of the sounds possible are important in any given language.

Rhythm is also important, so the child needs to practice sound combinations in the correct cadence. The child soon learns that some of the combinations evoke humorous responses from adults and make the child the center of attention—and who doesn't enjoy center stage! Once they develop a vocabulary, children themselves find delight in laughing at their own speech.

Later, humorous language use appears also to be the result of language development. Overextension of parts of speech role is common in preschoolers. For example:

> "Look! A sweep." (pointing to a broom)
> "Look, Mommy! Charlie's putting all his looseness in his neck." (Charlie is a cat.)

Or

> "Daddy's coming down the upstairs."

As with play activities of other types, our role as teacher with children should be that of encouraging language play. The following suggestions are helpful:

> Be prepared to laugh at your own verbalizations. Intentionally create puns and share language jokes and riddles with the child. Encourage language play by immersing yourself in it. Encourage the child to do likewise.
>
> Choose books and other materials that incorporate clever language play, verse, or riddles.
>
> Street riddles and chants and the sing-song verse for many playground games serve as language play. Encourage play activities and games that incorporate them.

Drawing

Drawing is a natural extension of play. In many respects it may be thought of as an expressive counterpart in which the child fulfills a need to represent reality—to both reduce it and extend it beyond what it appears to be by means of personal expression that incorporates language but also goes beyond it. Although play, in crude form, needs few if any readiness skills, drawing does require certain fundamental abilities before the child can proceed with those skills necessary for writing development. The following readiness inventory will be helpful in this area:

AN INFORMAL ASSESSMENT INVENTORY
FOR DRAWING-TO-WRITING READINESS

	YES	NO
1. The child can adequately hold a writing/drawing instrument, that is, pencil or crayon, and show reasonable control in drawing crude figures.	____	____

2. The child draws figures with all major body parts (trunk, head, arms, legs) in the appropriate place.   _____ _____

3. Drawings of figures contain body parts that are reasonably proportioned.   _____ _____

4. Given a simple copying task, for example, reproducing square, triangle, and circle, the child can make a reasonable copy.   _____ _____

5. The child can complete a trace-the-dots picture.   _____ _____

6. The child is interested in drawing on his or her own when there is access to necessary materials.   _____ _____

Keep in mind that this inventory is not designed to identify children ready for drawing. Many children are ready to begin drawing before they can meet these inventory requirements. However, they probably need additional experience and practice before they are ready to perform the kind of drawing that serves as a precursor to writing.

BASIC STROKES

The basic strokes required for handwriting in any *system are implicit in the natural drawing of all normal children.* They incorporate these strokes in their drawings of human figures and objects. This suggests the most important instructional principle we can use in drawing and early handwriting development with children, *that is, that the child should be provided with adequate materials and supplies and encouraged informally to draw freely and whenever the child desires.*

Other activities that will help to develop basic strokes critical to handwriting, as well as greater understanding and a growing conception of writing, are to be found in the following areas.

Tracing   Trace-the-dot pictures are helpful in developing skills basic to drawing. They are available in commercially prepared materials. In addition, they can be designed and constructed by the parent or educator. Choose a balanced array of materials that assure that the child will utilize all of the important strokes and movements—straight lines, angles, curves, circles, loops, and breaks.

Copying   Copying activities ought to be utilized in the same fashion as tracing. The parent or teacher should start with relatively simple activities, possibly copying basic geometric shapes and simply contoured figures. As with tracing, the activity is most rewarding when done at the child's instigation and when not done for overlong periods.

Mental picture copying   This is essentially a mnemonic (memory-related) activity. Describe a simple object—an apple or a watermelon, for example—and ask the child to draw it. Conversely, the child can draw something and ask you to identify it. These activities can be increased in complexity as the child develops skills in perceiving the relationships of mental images to representations on paper. Remember, this is probably the first in a series of *direct* skill development sequences designed to assist the child in *conceptualizing* as well as representing writing.

A few notes about this section of drawing:

1. Remember that tracing, copying, and mental picture copying are implicitly more structured activities than most considered so far. Therefore, attention span and interest are likely to be shorter. It is also more tempting to structure these activities in a more constraining fashion. Avoid this as much as possible. Encourage through provision of materials, suggestions, and personal interest by modeling the activity yourself.

2. At this stage, do not emphasize the functional value of the skills being developed. Let natural inclination and desire to please play a motivational role.

3. Maintain balance in the activities. Variety and balance provide a more likely interest base and are also in keeping with research findings suggesting that emphasis on one skill type or the other is inappropriate.

Pictography

Before the children engage in activities in pictography, they must be able to draw adequately to represent figures and objects in reasonable proportion and with all critical components present. If that skill is present, they are ready for pictography.

Pictography is the most important stage in the development of the child's perception of writing-as-conceptual-act. It serves as an important transition from drawing—representing personal interpretations of reality with pencil or crayon—to an abbreviated form of drawing that is sort of a shorthand in that what is drawn *stands* for something *other* than what is drawn. The child then partials out reality by leaving out critical representational features in the drawing. The drawing then *re-presents* rather than presents. The pictograph is a symbol that stands for something greater in both dimension and conception than itself. The child is in the process of shorthanding reality on paper by abbreviating with pencil. This is critical for the preschooler. The preschool child *must* understand that marks on paper can be greater in representational potential than that from which they derive and, possibly, than that for which they stand.

Redrawing   Present reasonably detailed drawings of figures and ask the child to draw copies. Include a range of topics relevant to the child's interests. As the child's skills increase, select more detailed drawings for duplication. On occasion allow the child to have only a brief time to study a given drawing, then remove it from view and ask the child to draw it as he or she remembers it to be. Be especially careful in providing an unpressured gamelike atmosphere, and do not frustrate the child by pressing for detail. In fact, the purpose of this activity is to encourage the child to abbreviate drawings. Ask the child to describe the original picture based upon his or her own reproduction. Encourage the child to see that the point of this game is not so much to draw an exact duplicate as to use drawing as a mnemonic cue to the original.

Mental image drawing   After the child is comfortable with the Redrawing activities, provide a verbal description of a scene and ask the child to draw it. Again, begin with simple scenes and progress to more intricate ones. For example, suggest ''a ball lying on the ground with a ball bat'' or ''a wagon.'' Then progress to scenes including humor and animal figures. Talk about the child's work. Provide positive comments about how well he or she remembered the things you described and could talk about them even when the details were not included in the drawings.

Pictographs as mnemonics for ideas   After successfully performing the preceding activities, the child is ready to utilize drawings as pictographs for more abstract ideas. Tell the child that you are going to say four or five different things and that he or she should use pencil and paper in any way that will aid in remembering, because that is the object of the game. We are not interested in the preciseness of the drawings or marks, or whether they look like the object or idea, but how helpful they are in serving as cues to the child for remembering what was told.

Begin by using the mental image activity as a base. Start with concrete objects, for example, a basketball or a wagon. Then move to more detailed objects, for example, a tree or a big dog. Next, include multiple objects and action verbs that suggest relationships, for example, a cow following a girl or a man pulling a wagon. *Insert specific numbers and color adjectives in your groups (remember quantity and color cues are very helpful to the child in using pictographs as cues),* for example, the very *white* feathers or *four* dogs on a street. Finally, increase the range of options and provide gradually for more abstract ideas, for example, the bug has 1,000 legs or the rain fell on a very dark night.

Notice that for ''the bug has 1,000 legs'' the child is likely to respond that he or she cannot draw that many legs. Suggest that he or she might make just a few legs but then remember that that means there were a thousand.

Assertions of feelings, beliefs, and likes or dislikes are the most demanding, for they provide few concrete objects that the child can tie pictographs to. The physical resemblance of the symbol to the thing or idea for which it stands becomes less significant.

Remember that these activities can frustrate the child if they are too difficult or inappropriately timed. Present them as a game for fun. They can be done one-on-one or with groups of children. With small groups there is excellent opportunity for the children to talk about each other's pictographs and why some are different from others. Regardless of whether the teacher or parent is working with one child or a group, discussion about the pictographs and sharing of ideas are important. Writing development feeds on oral language.

Ideography

Pictographs have major limitations as symbols. They tend to be tied more to things, objects, and ideas than to relationships between them. They are time-consuming to produce. But most importantly our society is committed to the letters of the alphabet as written language symbols. Therefore, the child needs to learn to recognize letters and reproduce letters in writing in order to function as a literate person. Reproducing letters must ultimately be considered as part of handwriting. Our primary concern at this point is with the child's conceptualization of ideograph (letter) as symbol.

Writing the alphabet There are a variety of commercially produced trade books for teaching letters of the alphabet. These range from picture books that help the child recognize the letters in both capital and lower-case form to tracing and/or copy-consumable books where the child is taught to reproduce the letters. The teacher should undertake activities such as these concurrently; that is, children should be given practice in reproducing letters of the alphabet as soon as they learn to recognize them.

The teacher should keep in mind that, although children do need to learn to pronounce the letters of the alphabet, they *should not* be taught that letter sounds correspond to word sounds in our language. There is some relationship but a limited one. There are 26 letters in the alphabet but anywhere from 42 to 60-odd sounds in our words, depending on which linguistic authority you consult. Long *a* such as that in "lay" corresponds to the sound of the letter *a*. However, the *a* in "ball" does not. The letter *t* seldom finds expression as a sound in English, with the exception of a word like "tee" or "tea." It often appears with *h* to produce the sound of *th* in "this" or a different *th* as in "think"; one is said to be a voiced sound, the other unvoiced. The important point is that the letter-sound correspondence of words in print is not as simple or straightforward as simply sounding out the alphabet.

A second matter that must be considered is that there are a variety of approaches to handwriting instruction in the schools from kindergarten through the third grade and sometimes beyond. Most children move from a form of block printing to cursive writing, perhaps most often in the second grade. However, there appear to be an increasing number of systems that are based on cursive writing from the start.

For the preschooler, the system to be employed later should not be a concern. Initial practice in maintaining a steady flow of curves, angles, and straight lines joined as occurs in early scribble writing provides fine motor skill practice and a base for cursive expression, as well as some conceptualization of what writing is for and about.

Ideograph as mnemonic After the child has learned the alphabet, selected whole words can be learned through association with pictures or drawings. Again, there are a number of high-quality trade books with this feature. Activities such as those in the section on pictography provide an opportunity for the child to begin to associate words in print with ideas in oral language. Again, as with other activities in the symbolizing strand, be very careful not to frustrate children by initiating them into these experiences until they are ready. Observe carefully their free-time employment of books and their activities with pencil or crayon and paper. Common sense and sensitivity to the child's feelings and needs are sufficient for the teacher to know the level and kind of pictographic or ideographic activities possible.

In music   There are many reasons for music in the life of the young child other than its contribution to writing development. Our concerns, however, are in the latter area. First, sense of rhythm is critical to writing. The feel for the ebb and flow of words and ideas is keyed to rhythm and its employment. Second, music coheres. Notes alone do not make music. It is only in their combination that meaning evolves. The same is true of writing. And, third, there is a grammar to music, an internal structure whose elements of transition and logic are analogous to those in writing. Rhythm, coherence, and internal structure provide a critical conceptual core in music that can help the child in his or her efforts to develop writing skills and abilities. Music provides an excellent opportunity to enhance human relationships in a mode appreciated by all children. The roots of expression are perhaps most easily tapped by song.

Some general guidelines for utilizing music are:

Involve the child in music daily. Nursery rhymes are particularly appropriate with the very young.

Encourage the child to use musical instruments. Shakers can be made from empty containers, for example, cardboard oatmeal boxes with dried beans inside and taped shut. They can be used for listening and guessing games. Rhythm sticks of varying lengths and thicknesses are easily made from wooden dowels (waxing them increases the resonance). Musical bells of all sizes can be purchased reasonably. Bamboo rattles and "pipes" are easily made from bamboo rods.

Encourage rhythm games where children march or dance in time to music on records or to their own drums, tambourines, or other percussion.

In drama   Dramatic expression is fundamental to all of the language arts. It assists the child in a range of activities, from fine motor skill development to oral language development, from skill in organizing and presenting a cohesive narrative in either verbal or nonverbal form to the development of a sophisticated understanding of symbols and their employment. This is not even to mention other critical matters such as an enhanced sense of aesthetics and a heightened power of imagination.

For the young child who has yet to adopt the inhibitions of personal expression that often accompany maturation in our society, dramatic expression provides additional opportunity to try out ideas, experiment with feelings and behaviors in a setting where reality is temporary. Nothing is risked. If the idea does not fit or does not work for some reason, it hasn't cost anything.

Drama falls into essentially two categories, dramatic improvisation and dramatic interpretation. The difference is in the amount of direction or text provided. Creative drama, free elaboration of a topic or theme by physical movement with or without verbal accompaniment, is improvisation. The more direction provided, the closer we move to dramatic interpretation.

An example of puppetry use can help illustrate how the same subject can be shifted from one type of drama to the other.

The teacher can involve children in a range of dramatic experiences by providing more or less direction to the situation.

Initially, the very young child engages in dramatic play alone. And a great deal of this can continue by use of puppets or show-and-tell situations where the child is encouraged to express ideas dramatically for the parent or teacher. However, the ultimate power of dramatic expression comes when children work in pairs or slightly larger groups to express an idea or interpret a situation.

For the young child, a free but encouraging unstructured environment with ample array of costumes, old clothing, and shoes is enough to evolve into a dramatic production. There are additional activities, however, that will encourage the use of creative drama. Some suggestions follow.

Marching to sound   For very young children, marching or dancing to a drum or other simple beat is effective. They can skip, tiptoe, or slide-step as they please.

Pantomime   Early pantomime is simply pretending to be things—a giant, someone walking on hot coals or trying to handle a hot potato. In later stages, small groups of children can plan a joint pantomime—a train, with engine, cars, and caboose; three bears lost in the forest; baseball players on a team.

Enacting a narrative   After hearing a story, children assume parts and re-enact the narrative. This can be done initially without language. Later, dialogue can be added if desired.

Planning and producing a story   After a little practice, young children can dramatically plan and produce their own simple stories. Assistance may be required initially, including participation by the teacher.

Children should have the opportunity to perform in both improvisational and interpretive settings. If there is interest, performing their own play for an audience of adults and/or other children can be exciting for the performers as well as the audience. Remember, however, that our primary interest is in the instructional role of drama rather than its artistic aims, as important as they are.

The writing development framework for preschool children covers a variety of language activities in an integrated fashion, even when there is individual focus on particular subskills. Its general features are comprehensive, because the act of writing is one requiring comprehensive knowledge and skills. Yet, for that, the framework is liberal and flexible, an intended guide to instruction and learning

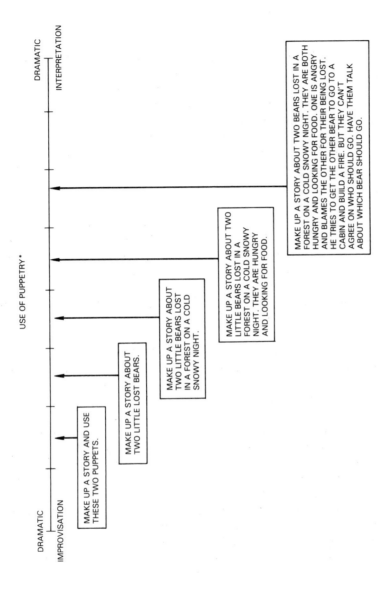

USE OF PUPPETRY*

DRAMATIC
IMPROVISATION

DRAMATIC
INTERPRETATION

MAKE UP A STORY AND USE THESE TWO PUPPETS.

MAKE UP A STORY ABOUT TWO LITTLE LOST BEARS.

MAKE UP A STORY ABOUT TWO LITTLE BEARS LOST IN A FOREST ON A COLD SNOWY NIGHT.

MAKE UP A STORY ABOUT TWO LITTLE BEARS LOST IN A FOREST ON A COLD SNOWY NIGHT. THEY ARE HUNGRY AND LOOKING FOR FOOD.

MAKE UP A STORY ABOUT TWO BEARS LOST IN A FOREST ON A COLD SNOWY NIGHT. THEY ARE BOTH HUNGRY AND LOOKING FOR FOOD. ONE IS ANGRY AND BLAMES THE OTHER FOR THEIR BEING LOST. HE TRIES TO GET THE OTHER BEAR TO GO TO A CABIN AND BUILD A FIRE. BUT THEY CAN'T AGREE ON WHO SHOULD GO. HAVE THEM TALK ABOUT WHICH BEAR SHOULD GO.

*From M. Klein, *Talk in the Language Arts Classroom* (Urbana, Ill.: National Council of Teachers of English, 1977). Reprinted by permission.

71

activities rather than a set of prescribed steps to be followed one after the other. Used with reason, good judgment, and sensitivity to the needs of the child, it can provide a substantial base for the development of writing in the young child.

RESOURCES FOR IDEAS AND ACTIVITIES FOR THE WRITING DEVELOPMENT FRAMEWORK

Strand 1—Oral Language

KLEIN, M. L., *Talk in the Language Arts Classroom.* Urbana, Ill.: NCTE/ERIC, 1977.
MOFFETT, J., and WAGNER, B. *Student-Centered Language Arts and Reading, K–13.* Boston: Houghton Mifflin, 1983.
TOUGH, J., *The Development of Meaning.* New York: John Wiley, 1977.
WEEKS, T. C., *Born to Talk.* Rowley, Mass.: Newbury House Publishers, 1979.
YAWKEY, T. D., and OTHERS. *Language Arts and the Young Child.* Itasca, Ill.: F. E. Peacock Publishers, 1981.

Strand 2—The Foundation Skills Network

KAMII, C., and DEVRIES, R. *Physical Knowledge in Preschool Education.* Englewood Cliffs, N.J.: Prentice-Hall, 1978.
LAVATELLI, C. S. *Piaget's Theory Applied to an Early Childhood Curriculum.* Cambridge: American Science and Engineering, Inc., 1970.
SHARP, E. *Thinking Is Child's Play.* New York: Avon Books, 1969.
VALLETT, R. E., *Developing Cognitive Abilities: Teaching Children to Think.* St. Louis: The C. V. Mosby Co., 1978.
BUTLER, A., and OTHERS. *Play As Development.* Columbus: Charles E. Merrill, 1978.
GARVEY, C., *Play.* Cambridge: Harvard University Press, 1977.
GILLIES, E., *Creative Dramatics for All Children.* Washington, D.C.: Association for Childhood Education International, 1972–1973.
GOODNOW, J., *Children Drawing.* Cambridge: Harvard University Press, 1977.
HENRY, M. W., *Creative Experiences in Oral Language.* Urbana, Ill.: NCTE, 1967.
MATTERSON, E. M., *Play with a Purpose for Under Sevens.* Harmondsworth, Middlesex, England: Penguin Books, 1975.

Writing Development Through the Elementary and Middle School Years

chapter

4

AN OVERVIEW

The child's writing ability develops significantly during the elementary school years. Indeed, it may be reasonable to assert that there is greater development during this time than at any other period in the child's education. Many children entering kindergarten can already form some letters of the alphabet. Others can write their name.

By the third-grade year, a number of dramatic changes have taken place in the child's writing. In terms of writing mechanics, manuscript and block printing have been replaced by cursive handwriting in nearly all cases. Fundamental mechanics such as punctuation and capitalization are in reasonable control. Children know something about paragraphing. And spelling appears more in line with that perceived as acceptable in the adult world. Perhaps of even greater interest, however, is that the child has begun to come to grips with writing-as-conceptual-act. The child has literally moved from an understanding that written symbols can be used to represent communicative intent on the part of the writer to a position of composer-author who can produce a variety of written messages.

During the intermediate and middle school years, the child refines the basic structures of written composition and develops new skills as well. By the intermediate grades, the child begins to recognize the need to relate the overall form and structure of the writing to the needs and characteristics of different audiences and to the different purposes for the writing. The child also begins to see that different styles, syntactic structures, and approaches to the writing task are required by different writing forms or modes.

Knowing these relationships and being able to handle the demands in writing, however, are two different things. Sophistication in relating style to purpose, audience, and discourse mode develops over time. And it is in the middle school years when the teacher can see the developing writer's first significant moves in utilizing the background of writing knowledge and skills that the learner brings to the classroom.

The quality of the written expression, its place of importance in the life of the child, and the extent to which later literacy skills develop are not simply a function of natural acquisition. What happens to and for the child in instructional settings determines such matters significantly. For this reason, it is extremely helpful to know what aspects of the writing process appear to be central to the child in the elementary grades. What factors appear to be consistent in the child's activities and thinking before, during, and after the writing act? What elements seem to be universal in their appearance in the writing of children in grades 1 through 8? Answering questions such as these places us in a much better position for designing both instructional materials and activities as well as an overall curriculum in composition for grades 1 through 8.

The research reviewed in the first part of this book indicates that we are beginning to discover answers to many of these questions. In addition, there is an increasing body of research focusing specifically upon the writer through the grades. We shall examine salient features of this research and generate a number of important governing principles for writing and writing instruction. Using this information, we shall offer a conceptual framework for composition instruction and development in the elementary/middle school years. Finally, we shall consider a variety of appropriate activities and techniques that can serve as effective vehicles for teaching writing during this period; vehicles that legitimately derive from an overall design constructed from theory, research, and successful teaching practices.

WHAT WE KNOW
ABOUT WRITING
DEVELOPMENT
IN GRADES 1 THROUGH 8

There are essentially two ways that we can consider writing development in the elementary/middle school grades. One is by examining the behaviors and processes of composing that the student goes through. Consider, for example, the kinds of physical or psychological conditions that best lend themselves to productive writing. Another is to consider the elements, skills, and concepts central to writing as a literate enterprise. For example, what features of paragraph structure must a writer consider and master in order to produce an acceptably written paragraph? What are the sentence building skills that are requisite?

Of course, in addition to these two ways of looking at writing development, there is also the matter of considering the merger of the two—the learner and the skills and concepts of writing. And, for the teacher, this is an area of critical concern, for when all else is said and done, effective instruction in written composition *must* place the learner and the learner's interests, experiences, and desires to communicate in the center of things.

We now have an expanding body of research that elaborates the above assertion considerably. Perhaps the most telling of this research in the early grades is that done by Don Graves during the early to mid-1970s, and which is currently being extended by Graves and other researchers.[1]

Graves's initial work focused upon the writing processes of 7-year-olds. Key findings in that research can be summarized in two categories, learning environments and performance differences between boys and girls.

I.   Learning Environments
   A.   Informal writing environments tend to elicit more writing and writing of greater length from first-grade children.
   B.   In informal learning environments, children appear to need much less external motivation and supervision in their writing.
   C.   Informal learning environments tend to help and encourage boys in writing, while girls can cope with either formal or informal environments more effectively.
   D.   Requiring large amounts of assigned writing in either type of learning environment inhibits the range, content sophistication, and amount of writing produced by children.
II.   Boy/Girl Differences in First-Grade Writing
   A.   Girls tend to write longer pieces than boys in either informal or formal writing environments.
   B.   Boys tend to do more unassigned writing than girls.
   C.   Boys seldom use the first person (I) in unassigned writing, but those who do tend to be the more developmentally advanced ones.
   D.   Boys write more about themes and ideas identified as secondary or focusing on strange or faraway places than do girls.
   E.   Girls, on the other hand, write more about primary territory themes—home and school—than do boys.
   F.   Boys tend to be more concerned about matters of spacing, letter formation, and neatness than are girls, although their productions do not necessarily reflect tangible results of this concern.
   G.   Girls appear to stress and utilize prethinking, organization, and feelings in characterizations, and provide more illustrations to support their judgments than do boys.

Most of Graves's findings are tied quite directly to the developmental level of most first-graders. Just in the process of moving into the stage of concrete operations cognitively and learning the abstracting character and potential of written language in its more general form and contours, first-grade children—and some second-grade children—are simply not capable of exhibiting the refinements central to mature writing. Note, however, that children by the intermediate grades are quite capable of adjusting to a formal learning environment and producing written expression that reflects the rhetorical devices of mature writing. And, by the middle school grades, more intricate and complex aspects of composition are ready to be learned.

The mature learner knows that the writer composes for different audiences—the self, the known or familiar "you," and the unknown "you." Each audience type requires the writer to adjust writing mood, vocabulary, and sentence structure accordingly. As the "psychological distance" increases from audience of self through audience of unknown you, the writer must increase the detail and level of formality. The ability to establish proper psychological distance between the self as writer and the various types of audience requires that the composer objectify the writing, that is, treat it as a thing apart, as an outside viewer would. This requires both skill and developmental maturity. Most first-graders and many second-graders do not yet have this facility.[2] Bound up in themselves, children at this age may reasonably be expected to write primarily for themselves regardless of the audience demands in any given specific writing situation.

Children in the primary grades tend to write in all forms (narrative, expository, and creative), and for all purposes (to inform, to persuade, and to entertain) in the same fashion regardless of the audience shifts that may occur. Children at this age are so thoroughly caught up in the content of their writing that they seem constant participants in the events and experiences of the writing. Little thought is given to formulating even rough notes or outlines prior to the writing.[3] There is no such thing as a "first draft" or "second draft" of a composition for these children. In their world there is only one draft, and they think of changes that might be made in that later as less a revision than an addendum, with little added for direct rhetorical improvement.

As a matter of fact, when we examine the writing of children at this level, we consistently find that they are totally immersed in the what of their compositions rather than the how or, for that matter, the why.[4] Events, activities, people, things, pets, and personal experiences are all one and the same, with writing still relatively unskilled and undisciplined.

This has important implications for prewriting activities. Playing, drawing, talking, and viewing all possess rich potential for generating a proper writing environment. In the primary grades, children should usually choose their own topics for writing from their background and experiences, because then their writing will be more prolific and of higher quality. Children should be permitted to rehearse or prepare for the writing experience through the activities discussed earlier. They should be allowed to change the direction of their writing while in the writing process, and they should be allowed to take physical breaks from their writing, that is, walk around. We must remember that during the writing process it is normal for people to write in spurts—brief periods of sustained production interrupted by contemplation and physical movement.

The gradual switch from total immersion in the content of the writing to a posture that allows the writer to consider writing as a construct in itself with words, sentences, paragraphs, and nearly infinite possibilities for combinations of these things to achieve different purposes for different audiences is an evolving one encompassing all of the elementary school experience.

By the fourth grade or so, children begin to recognize relationships between grammatical structures and modes of discourse.[5] By that time, for example, they use a greater quantity of more complex subordination in writing argument than they do in expository or in narrative writing. By the fourth grade, in fact, the most complex sentence structures used by children occur in argumentation, followed by exposition, narration, and simple description.

An examination of these various modes or forms of written expression suggests quite strongly that development of a variety of syntactic skills in writing is related to an exposure to writing experiences that requires the composer to produce in all modes rather than only one or two.

Developing syntactic or sentence structure skills constitutes a major area of concern for writing instruction in all the elementary grades. Sentence writing ability is perceived as the single most important skill in the writing instruction curriculum. Grammar is normally taught in every grade beginning with the third. This is so despite the lack of any conclusive connection between grammar and writing proficiency.

> Statistical and nonexperimental studies using correlation analysis by Hoyt, Rapeer, Boraas, Asher, Segal, and Barr, Catherwood, Bradford, and Robinson failed to show a significant relationship between grammatical knowledge and writing ability. Except for Wykoff's study, the experimental studies by Briggs, Symonds, Crawford and Royer, Cutright, Ash, Benfer, Clark, Warner and Guiler, Milligan, Frogner, Krause, Smith, and Maize also failed to support the case for grammar. After a tally of procedural and other limitations, the research still overwhelmingly supports the contention that instruction in formal grammar is an ineffective and inefficient way to help students achieve proficiency in writing.[6]

The above observation by Sherwin was concerned almost entirely with the applications of formal traditional grammar rather than more contemporary linguistic grammars. Further, most of these studies were based upon application of written instruction or drill/paper practice activities in grammar. However, research focusing upon verbal correction of children's "grammar" or, more accurately, their usage is also discouraging. Gleason, for example, concluded after a series of studies with first-, second-, and third-graders: "In listening to us, the children attended to the sense of what we said and not the form. And the plurals and past tenses they offered were products of their own linguistic systems, and not the imitations of us."[7]

More contemporary research examining the impact of informal grammar activities incorporating sentence-combining and sentence-building skills through the elementary grades has been very promising.[8] This research indicates quite clearly that sentence-combining activities, when incorporated within a more comprehensively conceived writing program, can succeed in enhancing children's syntactic fluency and sophistication more effectively than can programs not including them.

Note, however, the key reference to a "comprehensively conceived" composition program. The pattern of both theory and research suggests that a wide variety of factors must be taken into consideration in a writing curriculum. Singling out one area for focus such as spelling or grammar or punctuation or penmanship or creative writing is not likely to yield writers who are skilled in their craft. The process is far too complex to be encompassed by only one skill or ability. Further, strategies and techniques for teaching subskills or subskill sets such as vocabulary or syntax have still to be elaborated precisely enough to indicate whether they are most effectively learned in isolation or integrated with other language-using skills or both, or whether the matter is strictly learner-dependent. In view of this situation, the general position of professional educators is one that assumes the importance of both integrating language-using skills instruction while at the same time providing appropriate focused instruction in the various skill and subskill areas.

For example, Marlene and Robert McCracken note about spelling instruction:

> The key to a child's understanding and learning is his ability to apply what he has been taught. To learn to spell, a child writes daily because he has something to record that he wants to remember or because he has something he wants to say. He writes sentences and stories independently and applies his spelling abilities in a meaningful context.[9]

Or consider the argument by Collins for the importance of meaning in communication, which in turn, calls for the integration of language skills with meaning as the governing focal point: "A good deal of the task of the language teacher consists of getting students to use language to produce meaning, since meaning is what connects speaking and writing and the development of language skill."[10] Typical, too, is Lundsteen's observation that "the truism of interrelations among the language arts holds when examining children's composition."[11]

In short, the demands of day-to-day teaching in the elementary and middle grades as well as researchers' opinions indicate that the teacher should be committed to immediate practical applications in writing instruction. And that requires incorporating a variety of approaches and techniques.

GOVERNING PRINCIPLES

A number of governing principles deriving from our consideration of theory and research follow. These principles are accompanied by sets of implications for the classroom teacher. In addition, they serve as a basis of assumption for the writing curriculum design framework that follows in the next chapter.

Governing Principle 1

Children in the primary grades produce more and higher-quality writing when operating in an informal learning environment that permits them considerable freedom in choosing topics and defining their own strategies for completing the writing assignment. In order to bring this situation about, there are a number of things the classroom teacher can do.

1. Establish a "writing resource center" in a specific part of the room. This does not require a wide range of equipment or materials, nor even a large amount of space. Arranging a large table with chairs around it or several desks and chairs clustered in a corner or a special area designated by shelving or small room dividers will do. The writing resource center needs ample supplies of paper (both lined and unlined), writing utensils (including felt-tip pens, pencils, and crayons), rulers, and other similar supplies. Magazines, books, pictures, and cassette tapes and tape recorders with earphones may also be added. Ideally, a file cabinet with ideas and materials for topics, arranged according to themes such as holidays, is also excellent. Children should be encouraged to place ideas of their own in the files in appropriate places.

The writing center should be open for use by children on a regular basis throughout the school day rather than simply at special times for reward or for supplemental use. *It is critical that children in the primary grades come to see writing* not *as a supplementary literacy skill but rather as a primary part of their total language and communication process.*

2. Encourage children to write in a variety of settings—in the classroom, at home, with friends, and on trips. Be prepared to respond to the writing, but for the most part do not set rigid deadlines for a given written exercise. Restrict the number of formally assigned writing tasks you require, especially those which require that the child write on a specific topic or idea.

Certain forms of writing appear to be more conducive to informal writing than others. For example, keeping a diary or personal journal and writing personal letters specifically and just friendly letters generally all appear to elicit more productive and personally motivated writing than do other forms such as reports or business letters.

Creative and narrative writing appear to inspire more production than other modes such as exposition and argumentation, although, as we noted earlier, thoroughgoing practice in *all* such modes is important in the primary as well as later grades.

3. Work diligently to provide children with a variety of learning experiences that encourage individual pursuits and independent study. Projects calling for small-group efforts (three to five children per group) or the pairing of children to pursue an idea are excellent, for two reasons. First, the mode of operation itself encourages joint planning and topic elaboration, including peers motivating peers—an especially important practice to get established. Second, and perhaps even more important, incorporating learning activities such as these within the larger instructional setting is conducive to a more informal learning atmosphere and enhances classmate rapport, helping to create an environment more supportive of writing development in the primary grades.

4. Make special efforts to incorporate dramatic activities into regular class-

room instruction. In addition to allowing, even encouraging, the physical movement so necessary to young children, drama provides unique opportunities to mix physical and mental knowledge of things, ideas, and feelings. Children have the chance not only to rehearse the known of their experiences but to project new possibilities without risk of commitment that would take them beyond the present. In effect, they can generate a new experience base for the content of their future writing.

Further, although effective drama may well be one of the more demanding modes of written discourse in its expressive potential, if we think of it simply as an opportunity to assist children—as a learning device for improving written expression—then our options are wide indeed. For, in addition to teaching the basic elements of a story grammar—that is, establishing a setting, developing characterizations of a protagonist and antagonist, and following a plot from initiating event through conflict elaboration and resolution to climax and dénouement—writing drama assists the child in growth of imagination, aesthetic sensitivity, and cooperative involvement with others.

Governing Principle 2

Children in the primary grades turn inward for the content of their writing. Personal experiences and immediate family and friends are the critical root sources of their writing.

Children plunge themselves into the objects and events in their lives *through* their words and sentences and *not* by *using* the words and sentences. The Russian psychologist Luria referred to this type of language operation as the "glass theory." According to this theory, children are only tangentially aware of the words and sentences as language constructs in themselves. Instead, their object representation, which is the content of their writing, is the dominant aspect of their writing, reading, or speaking.

Of course, in order to be an effective writer, the child must come to see that close control of vocabulary, syntax, and other external linguistic elements is central to good writing. The task of the primary grades teacher, then, is twofold. First, the circumstances of the writing situation should be structured so as to capitalize on the child's experience base. In other words, activities and writing development strategies need to focus primarily upon the everyday events in children's lives.

Second, however, activities and language instruction strategies and techniques need to be designed so that children begin to develop a sense of language structure and form. Children need to have practice in manipulating language both in order to see the variations in effect achieved by doing so and simply for the play aspects of doing so. Ultimately, our success as writing instructors partly depends upon our recognizing that the building of a repertoire of syntactic and semantic options is critical to effective writing. The writer must develop a *conscious* realization of what those syntactic and semantic choices are for any given writing situation. The merger of appropriate structural and vocabulary choices with the content of the writing and the demands of the circumstances may well be the final measure of style and quality writing competence. And, in order to bring such a merger about, the writer must become a controlling manipulator of as many linguistic options as possible.

In a later chapter we shall offer a variety of activity types that are designed to help children begin this important skill development process.

Governing Principle 3

Learners should see composition as consisting of three important phases— prewriting, writing, and revision. These three phases need to be incorporated throughout the instructional program, including grades 1 through 8.

Prewriting activities are important for all writers. Revision, or follow-up activities to the writing, remains a problem for writers of all age categories, according to the National Assessment of Educational Progress.[12] Many writers see revision as a mechanical process of correcting spelling, punctuation, and capitalization without concern for content or writing style. The result of such a perception is that revision often turns out to be a waste of time. This, in spite of the fact that revision should be highly fruitful for both improving the quality of the written product and developing writing skills in the student.

Throughout the grades, writing should be regarded as a three-phase operation. A positive attitude should be taken toward all three activities—prewriting, writing, and revision—and adequate time must be given to all three. There may occasionally be some writing that does not warrant revision. The writing perhaps simply should be set aside. However, that should be a rare occurrence, and, in most cases, the student should become so accustomed to revision as to see it simply as a natural part of the writing act.

In fact, instilling a sense of writing as a nonending accumulative process whose open-ended character is to be accepted and even enjoyed must be a major early goal in the writing program. And, perhaps, of all the aspects of this writing process, none is more important or demanding of the teacher's creative planning skills than the prewriting phase.

Governing   inciple 4

Writing serves different purposes—to inform, to describe, to explain, to persuade or argue, to entertain—none of which are age-specific. Beginning writers, older children, and adult writers alike employ writing for these purposes. It is only the degree of sophistication that differs and not the range or general character of the purposes.

In considering the strategies and techniques possible in teaching writing, the teacher needs to anticipate possible writing situations carefully so that experience in writing for different purposes is assured. In many cases, this can be done implicitly. For example, when students are given a problem to resolve in a small-group environment with a written "report" anticipated, the result will almost assuredly be primarily an exercise in written persuasion. Many of us overuse one writing purpose or another in structuring writing activities for students. For example, creative writing is important, but so are descriptive and persuasive writing. Writing to inform is basic to a good composition program; however, if children write only to inform, they will miss the opportunity to develop skills unique to the other writing purposes. Oral and written language are aspects of the same communication process, and the same purposes hold in both oral discourse and writing.[13]

Governing Principle 5

Writing occurs in many different forms—stories, poems, essays, journals, notes, letters, reports, scripts for plays. These forms incorporate a more limited number of discourse modes—exposition, narration, argumentation, and fiction.

Both forms and discourse modes are factors that bear directly on the decision making teachers must do in developing a writing program. Grammatical and semantic complexity factors, for example, correlate with discourse mode type. Generally speaking, simplified exposition (writing to describe or explain) is less complex than narration (more extended description from a subjective viewpoint), and narration is less complex than argumentation. Argumentation is the most grammatically and semantically complex of the discourse modes. It is distinguished by greater resort to subordination, conditional (if-then) clauses, and hypothetical or suppositional language.

However, it is only at the end of the third grade or beginning of the fourth grade that children really begin recognizing relationships between grammatical structures and modes of discourse.[14] In writing argument, they begin to use more complex subordination, and in greater quantities, than in either exposition or narrative writing.

It is reasonable to assume that a greater proportion of writing time in the primary grades should be given to creative writing activities, an area where children can incorporate personal experiences and the motivating power of storytelling. During the intermediate and middle school grades there should be an increasing attention to exposition and argumentation as writing modes. All modes of writing should receive attention in all grades. However, emphasis shifts somewhat toward the logical and analytical writing demands as the learner matures.

Governing Principle 6

The writer writes for different audiences, which we earlier identified as the self, the known or personal you, and the unknown you. During the intermediate school years, students need to develop necessary skills in adapting written structure and content to context and audience.

These three audience types comprise the readers of writing. Since they are in different settings and relate differently to the writer, their needs and demands as readers will also differ dramatically. When we write for ourselves, a few scribbled notes or even signs or pictographs will usually suffice. However, as the psychological distance increases, as we begin to deal with an unknown you audience, for example, we must provide more detail, explanation, and formality so that there is less risk of obscurity or ambiguity in our writing. The effective writer is sensitive to the different types of audience and adjusts the writing style and content to fit the unique demands of each audience type.

This ability to establish appropriate psychological distance between the self as writer and a given audience requires that the writer be able to move out of an egocentrically centered view of reality, something preoperational children cannot do. Most kindergarten and first-grade children are likely to lack the ability to stand back mentally and look at their writing as an outside viewer, as one apart from the writing even though it is theirs.[15] Bound up in their own language use and thought, they tend to write primarily for themselves regardless of the demands of the writing situation.

In the early part of the primary grades, children should be allowed to be productive writers first, regardless of audience. During the intermediate and middle school years, instruction should incorporate different audience demands and students need to consciously consider implications for their writing.

Governing Principle 7

Students should write often.

Quantity of writing alone does not assure quality or even proficiency in writing. It is easy enough to simply go through the mechanics of writing without real involvement, a personal immersion in the act that is at the heart of being a good writer. However, insufficient writing practice can defeat even the best possible composition instruction. Students need to write daily in order to develop important writing skills and to inculcate a sense of pride and joy in writing as a personal means of expression. This need not mean a lengthy composition, story, poem, or journal entry every day. It means, in some cases, writing a short paragraph or even just a sentence or two. Playing with word order in a sentence, examining the implications of adding a particular word or deleting one, and trying various placements of a sentence in different parts of a paragraph or story are all useful experiences central to effective composition instruction.

The most important point to keep in mind regarding this particular governing principle is that *all* writing experiences should have potential for motivating students. Ideally, the student should perceive that writing is something personally valued by the teacher. The effective teacher of composition is one who is also a practitioner of the craft of writing. The teacher should engage in much of the same writing that children are asked to do. Writing stories, poems, plays, letters, reports all fall within the range of important activities here.

In addition to personally exhibiting the inportance of writing in his or her own life, the teacher, by engaging in writing, is able to maintain more easily a sensitivity to the challenges of writing as well as its pleasures. We too easily forget that, although writing truly is a labor of love, it is labor nonetheless, labor that is physically and mentally demanding. In short, when it comes to writing, the teacher should never ask of the student more than the teacher would be willing to do.

These governing principles and their implications constitute the underlying assumptions of the elementary school program in writing instruction, which will be detailed in the next chapter. A writing curriculum framework is then proposed that is designed to achieve the objectives of a quality composition program.

NOTES

1. D. Graves, "An Examination of the Writing Processes of Seven Year Old Children," *Research in the Teaching of English,* 9 (Winter 1975): 227–41; and D. DeFord, ed., *Learning to Write: An Expression of Language* (Columbus: The Ohio State University, Summer 1980).

2. J. Piaget, *The Language and Thought of the Child* (New York: New American Library, 1955); L. Vygotsky, *Thought and Language* (Cambridge, MIT Press, 1962); and L. Vygotsky, *Mind in Society* (Cambridge: Harvard University Press, 1978).

3. W. Petty, "The Writing of Young Children," in *Research on Composing: Points of Departure,* eds. C. Cooper and L. Odell (Urbana, Ill.: National Council of Teachers of English, 1978).

4. Graves, "Examination of the Writing Processes," 227–41; D. Graves, "Research Update," *Language Arts,* 56 (October 1979): 829–35; Petty, "The Writing of Young Children"; J. Moffett and B. Wagner, *Student-Centered Language Arts and Reading K–13* (Boston: Houghton Mifflin, 1976); and R. Hillerich, "Developing Written Expression: How to Raise—Not Raze—Writers," *Language Arts,* 56 (October 1979): 769–77.

5. J. Perron, "Changing the Question: Psycholinguistics and Writing" (paper presented at the Conference on English Education, Minneapolis, 1978); and M. Klein, "Teaching Writing in the Elementary Grades," *The Elementary School Journal,* 81 (May 1981): 319–26.

6. S. Sherwin, *Four Problems in Teaching English: A Critique of Research* (Scranton: International Textbook Co., 1969).

7. C. Cazden, *Child Language and Education* (New York: Holt, Rinehart & Winston, 1972).

8. D. Bateman and F. Zidonis, *The Effects of a Study of Transformational Grammar on the Writing of Ninth and Tenth Graders* (Champaign: National Council of Teachers of English, 1966); J. Mellon, *Transformational Sentence Combining: A Method for Enhancing the Development of Syntactic Fluency in English Composition* (Champaign: National Council of Teachers of English, 1969); F. O'Hare, *Sentence Combining: Improving Student Writing Without Formal Grammar Instruction* (Urbana: National Council of Teachers of English, 1973); and W. Combs, "Further Effects of Sentence-Combining Practice on Writing Ability," *Research in the Teaching of English,* 10 (Fall 1976): 137–49.

9. M. McCracken and R. McCracken, *Reading, Writing and Language: A*

Practical Guide for Primary Teachers (Winnepeg: Penguin Publishers, 1979), pp. 52–53.

10. B. Kroll and R. Vann, eds., *Exploring Speaking-Writing Relationships: Connections and Contrasts* (Urbana: National Council of Teachers of English, 1981).

11. S. W. Lundsteen, ed., *Help for the Teacher of Written Composition (K–9): New Directions in Research* (Urbana: National Council of Teachers of English/ERIC, 1976).

12. "National Assessment of Educational Progress, *National Assessment of Educational Progress Newsletter,* 10, No. 5 (October 1977).

13. M. Klein, "Designing a Talk Environment for the Classroom," *Language Arts,* 56 (September 1979): 647–56.

14. Perron, "Changing the Question."

15. Piaget, *Language and Thought;* Vygotsky, *Thought and Language;* Vygotsky, *Mind in Society.*

Designing a Writing Curriculum for Grades 1 Through 8

chapter

5

After considering what research, theory, and teaching practice suggest, one may identify a number of characteristics reflected by teachers, children, and writing programs. These attributes may be viewed as defining a quality composition program.

1. *Writing is an integral part of the total program.* Composition lessons and activities are built into the school day. And, although much of this takes place within the block of instructional time typically referred to as "language arts/reading," the effective program places writing in a central role in the *entire* curriculum.

2. *The writing program reflects balance in its priorities between fluency development and skill/concept instruction. Research and practice, however, reveal that writing development will not occur satisfactorily in programs where fluency—consistent ongoing writing production—is not emphasized.* This is especially important in the primary grades, although fluency should be emphasized throughout all grades. Journal writing is a powerful instructional tool for this reason, in addition to having potential for improving narrative writing, a critical mode for all writers. However, instruction focusing on skills and rhetorical concepts is also important if quality writing is to result.

3. *The writing program reflects comprehensiveness in its attention to* all *important components of writing and writing instruction.* An effective program in

written composition makes every effort to assure that students develop skills in *all* forms of writing and for all writing purposes and functions.

4. *Writing is* taught *rather than merely assigned.* Practice alone is not effective. Although students throughout the grades should be encouraged to write on impulse, there also need to be a designated time and specified content for instruction in the various requisite skills.

5. *Instruction in writing attends to both "writing-as-mechanical-act" and "writing-as-conceptual-act."* Handwriting and the mechanics of writing are important. However, boring compositions correctly punctuated and written with elegant penmanship still remain dull. The teacher in a quality writing program helps children realize that *both* content and form are important in written expression.

6. *Students are allowed ample in-class writing time.* By encouraging writing as part of the regular school day and as something done throughout the day rather than as only part of the language arts time block, the teacher lets students know that writing skills are universally valued and not simply schooltime survival aids.

7. *There is a general agreement among teachers on how to evaluate or respond to students' writing.* Although teachers may respond differently to various children's writing, there should be a general consensus on what types of responses students should anticipate and receive.

8. *The writing program reflects staff curriculum development efforts rather than just basal textbook content.* Even the best basal programs are limited in what they can do in teaching writing. Often they overemphasize mechanics to the detriment of instruction in composing. Further, the very personal nature of the writing act should indicate the importance of day-to-day experience and personal involvement.

9. *Individual student progress is monitored and records are maintained in personal file folders.* The identification of important skills and the student's progress in them is important for both individualizing instruction and providing input and background information to the student's next teacher. The files should include samples of student writing.

10. *Instruction about grammar and other aspects of language structure and usage reflects an agreed-upon policy regarding their relationship to writing and their role in the curriculum. The language young children bring to, and initially use in, their writing must be both accepted and respected regardless of appropriateness for the task at hand.* The development of language-use skills—both oral and written—is an evolutionary process. A well-sequenced and articulated curriculum in written communications throughout the school years will ultimately determine writing facility. Each teacher along the way works toward its fulfillment but does not perform miracles. Steady incremental improvement in many of the more subtle skills of writing requires time and increasing maturity.

11. *Teachers are active practitioners of the craft of writing in their personal and professional lives.* We teach best what we enjoy and do best. More important, however, for writing instruction, the individual who writes regularly is more likely to be sensitive to its challenges as well as its potentials.

WRITING PROGRAM
OBJECTIVES FOR GRADES 1
THROUGH 8

The attributes of a quality writing program must be consistent with the governing principles generated by research, theory, and practice. For example, the first attribute of "comprehensiveness" is quite explicit in governing principles encouraging the need for attention to the varying purposes and functions of writing. As an additional step, we need to identify objectives that can specifically serve as benchmarks for program design.

The following objectives are intended to assist the teacher and curriculum leader in developing a program based on the principles generated by research, theory, and practice and, further, to place the program among those who practice top-quality instructional techniques.

Student Attitude and Performance
Objectives in Written Composition

1. *Students perceive all writing—whether giving directions, composing a poem, or describing an event—as creative.*

Writing is more than sensory-motor coordination. It is an active intellectual pursuit that draws upon all of our mental abilities. In some sense, even a brief written directive is creative, the result of mental-physical coordinations of the highest order.

2. *Students use personal experience as a basis for their writing, and they appreciate the significance of the commonplace in providing ideas for composition.*

Experience need not mean travel to distant places, trips to cultural centers, or even unusual personal events. A walk in the park, a picnic, a trip to the grocery store all represent an incredible array of rich experiences the writer can draw upon. It is not so much the development of experiences that is central but rather the development of our sensibilities and what they can do for us. The ability to perceive, fathom, store, and retrieve—then rework or refashion where necessary—is where personal experiences are involved in writing.

3. *Students understand the various reasons for writing and the functions of the written word.*

They learn that writing for communication is important. However, they, too, should reflect an understanding and utilization of writing in other functional ways as well—writing for self-expression, for example. This should become increasingly apparent in their approach to the writing act as well as in their feelings about the writing of others as they progress through the grades.

4. *Students confer with the teacher and/or peers when appropriate prior to, during, and after the writing act.*

The importance of language interaction, oral and written, has been consistently stressed. Students need to carry on dialogue with teachers, with other students, and with self before, after, and occasionally during the writing. Pedagogically, student-teacher conferences provide the most practical and attractive method for individualizing instruction in writing. Dialogue helps to sharpen awareness and heighten sensitivities to alternative avenues of expression. When done in an evaluative setting, it assists the student in developing the positive self-critical sense so important for producing writing of quality.

5. *Students are competent in a variety of composition types.*

Students learn how to size up the writing situation—consider audience, purpose, setting, and subject—and they adopt a writing style and writer's stance consistent with the writing situation. They are able to write effectively in the major modes of written expression—expository, narrative, and creative.

6. *Students develop an overall plan and an appropriate procedure for accomplishing any given writing task.*

To a certain extent, it is true that thinking takes place as each word alights on paper. However, it is also the case that effective writing requires considerable self-discipline and effective planning. Prewriting activities initially in the primary grades will largely be sharing orally about personal experiences, guided activities in effective use of senses, and oral dictation of stories. However, students should become increasingly proficient in task formulation, observation, data acquisition and organization, and outlining of the prospective composition, story, or play as they progress through the later grades.

7. *Students participate in daily writing activities with necessary time devoted to motivation, direction, and follow-up.*

This objective speaks to two areas of concern—the actual writing and both pre- and postwriting activities. Although the type, quantity, and purpose of the writing will vary greatly, consistent and regular involvement in writing is crucial. There should be, however, only a general pattern with considerable variety in when and how the writing is done. For example, some weeks might have irregular quantities of writing. One week might be devoted to working on one poem with two or three days of prewriting experiences and motivational activities built in. Other days might feature production of a single sentence with major discussion and consideration of how it might be rewritten. The important point is that in a quality program there are consistent and productive writing experiences.

8. *Students observe the amenities of spelling, usage, mechanics, and other manuscript conventions in writing.*

These are things that impact on the reader. Though not as mentally draining as the other aspects of writing, these "details" are still very important for acceptable and effective communication. Students need to develop an awareness of this importance and reflect enough concern for the appearance of their final written products to attend closely to such details.

A Composition Curriculum Framework for Grades 1 through 8

The concept of "comprehensiveness" has been referred to often in the literature review, in the governing principles formulated, and in the writing program objectives. In order to work toward developing appropriate activities and techniques for achieving this concept, it is important that we take an overall look at the various components and elements that define the content of a curriculum in composition. These are presented in "A Composition Curriculum Framework," which can be used as a curriculum design base for developing techniques and activities in composition and which will help the classroom teacher achieve the writing objectives formulated earlier in this chapter. A schematic of the framework is shown in Table 5–1.

There are essentially three sets of concepts or skills that the student must address and ultimately master: presentational amenities, elements of writing, and impinging factors of circumstance.

The first of these consists of the surface features of the written product in its final form for presentation to the reader. The presentational amenities enter into the writing act itself in only minimal and, usually, indirect fashion. Mastering the skills and concepts of presentational amenities is, in some senses, secondary to the development of composition skills. For example, attractive penmanship and excellent spelling abilities play no part in making a student a "good" writer. They are simply aspects of the written product that make it more attractive and presentable to the reader. However, since the ultimate goal of most writing is to communicate with another, this means that the presentational amenities are important to the writing program and deserve adequate attention. These presentational amenities fall into three categories—mechanics, style, and modes of discourse. They all have in common the important characteristic that each contributes in outward appearance to the composition, each helps to define the quality of the composition.

PRESENTATIONAL AMENITIES

Mechanics

There are four major subcategories of mechanics—handwriting, spelling, punctuation, capitalization. Each of these has certain unique features. For example, handwriting skills are largely a matter of fine motor coordination development. Capitalization is primarily a matter of memorization. Punctuation, though requiring some memorization, also requires some knowledge of grammar as well as some rhetorical judgment. Spelling is the most intellectually demanding of these skills. Sense of the phonology of the language (its sound system) and its grapheme (written signs or alphabet) and phoneme (individual significant sounds) relationships is necessary in order to spell accurately.

These distinctions between the subcategories are important. For one thing, they help to illustrate why a great deal of the skill of handwriting, punctuating, and capitalizing can be learned successfully within the larger context of the writing act. That is, many of these skills are developed as one practices and engages in writing as a whole. And, although this is also true of spelling to a limited extent, spelling most clearly of all these skills needs focused instruction and practice.[1]

TABLE 5–1. A Composition Curriculum Framework, Grades 1–8

PRESENTATIONAL AMENITIES	ELEMENTS OF WRITING	IMPINGING FACTORS OF CIRCUMSTANCE
I. *Mechanics*	I. *Syntax (Structure)*	I. *Audience*
Handwriting	A. Sentence Structure	Self
Spelling	Parts of speech	Personal You
Punctuation	Coordination	Unknown You
Capitalization	Predication	II. *Setting*
II. *Style*	Modification	Ceremonial
Usage choices	Subordination	Formal
Vocabulary choices	B. Paragraph Structure	Informal
Structure choices	Thesis/Body/Conclusion	Intimate
	Abstraction Levels	III. *Subject*
		Animate/Inanimate
	II. *Uses of Language*	Abstract/Concrete
	A. Nonasserting	Abstract/Specific
	Questioning (inquiring)	Personal/Nonpersonal
	Exclaiming	IV. *Purpose*
	Directing	To inform
	B. Asserting	To describe
	Describing	To explain
	Explaining	To inquire
	Proposing (arguing)	To direct
	III. *Logic of Language*	To persuade
	Sequence	To enjoy
	Unity/Coherence	

III. *Modes of Discourse (forms)*

Expository   argumentative (persuasive)
  reportive

Narrative   within fiction
  within
  nonfiction

Creative   drama
  prose   poetry

However, there should be focused instruction and practice in all these mechanical skills. In addition, they should be taught within the larger context of the written composition, although not at the expense of the content of the composition.

Style

There are three subcategories of Style—usage, vocabulary choice, and sense of appropriateness in structure and form choices.

As part of the writing program, students need to develop a strong sense of appropriateness in language use. In fact, an important underlying principle in all language instruction throughout the grades should be that the notion of appropriateness is more valid than the notion of correctness. For example, there are virtually no usage choices that would not be appropriate in a given context. Students should learn to use standard English effectively in their speech and writing. However, they should also have a repertoire of other types and choices and the knowledge of which to use in which context. More important, approaching usage and vocabulary choices in writing from the standpoint of appropriateness rather than correctness is a more positive teaching strategy in that it does not have incorrectness as an opposite alternative.

As with the mechanics subcategory to some extent, skill in selection of appropriate usage and vocabulary develops most effectively within the larger context of composition production. The same is true for sentence and paragraph structure choices. As students write and talk with peers and teachers about their writing, they have opportunities for seeing the importance of the various presentational amenities in contributing to the overall effectiveness of their writing. Thus there is a motivation for mastering these aspects of written language that is nearly impossible to duplicate in workbook and drill sheet activities.

This is not to say that practice, as well as selective instruction, should not incorporate such activities. They play an important role in providing focused instruction in specific subskills. However, variety, balance, and a realistic view of their strengths and limitations should be maintained.

Modes of Discourse (Forms)

Our composition curriculum framework identifies three major forms of writing in the presentational amenities strand.

Expository writing is that which essentially informs, describes, explains, or argues from a reasonably objective viewpoint. We break it into two subcategories here, reportive and argumentative. Reportive writing is that which conveys information, description, or explanation without personal judgment. It can describe a setting, person, object, situation, event, or some combination of all of these. In the primary grades children use exposition often in show-and-tell activities, in reports on events or activities to the rest of the class, or in giving directions to another on how to play a game or get to one's home. In the intermediate and middle school grades, exposition can appear in the form of book reports or descriptions of trips or experiences.

Figures 5–1 through 5–5 are typical examples of expository/reportive writing at various grade levels.

Kristie
I haveadog.
She is nice.
I sleep with her.
Her name is Patty.
She eats dog food.
I have a present for my
dog.

Grade 1

Figure 5–1.

Melissa
I have a little cat her name is
Nelly. I can feed her. I like to
play with her. She likes to
sleep on my bed.

Grade 2

Figure 5–2.

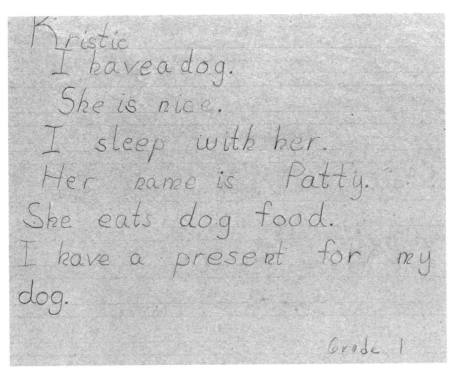

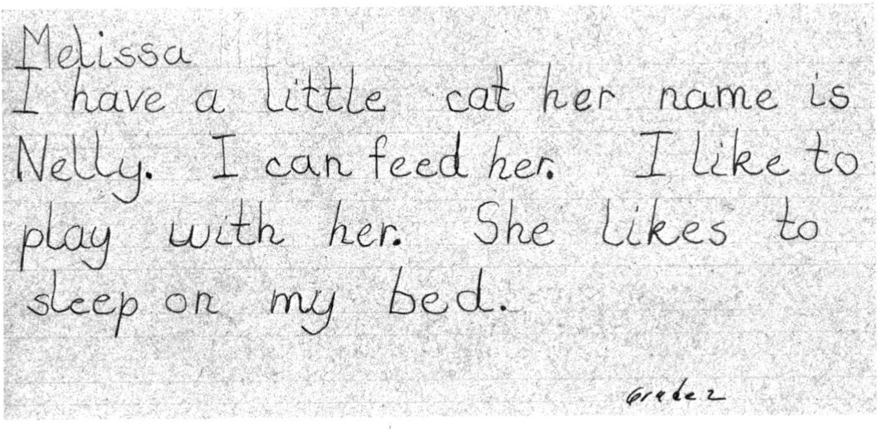

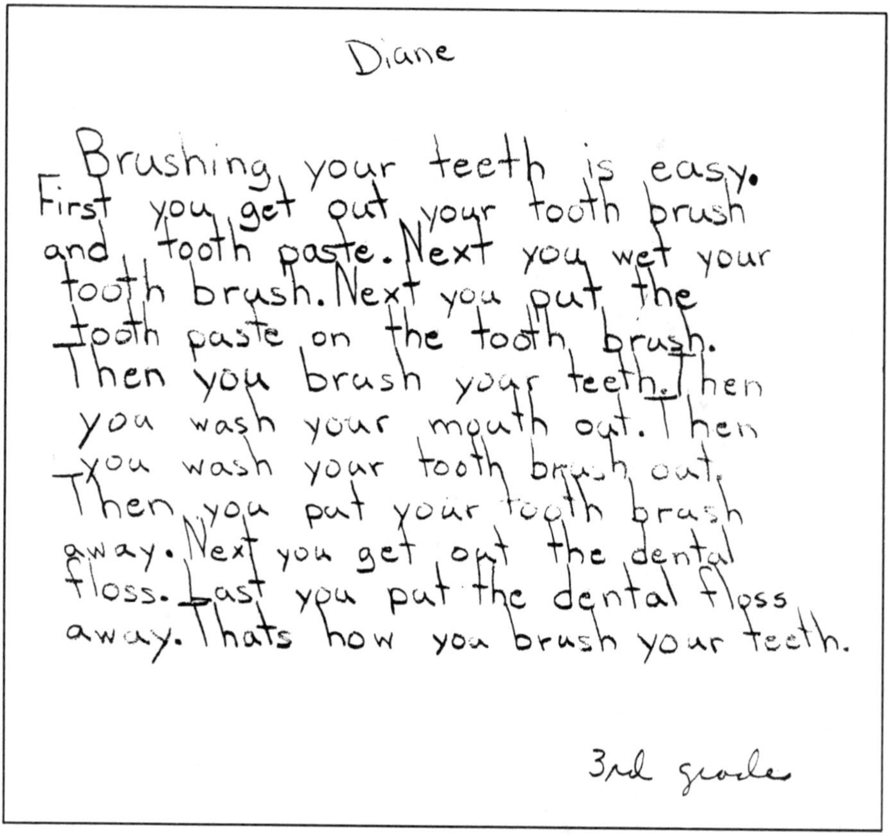

Diane

Brushing your teeth is easy.
First you get out your tooth brush
and tooth paste. Next you wet your
tooth brush. Next you put the
tooth paste on the tooth brush.
Then you brush your teeth. Then
you wash your mouth out. Then
you wash your tooth brush out.
Then you put your tooth brush
away. Next you get out the dental
floss. Last you put the dental floss
away. Thats how you brush your teeth.

3rd grade

Figure 5-3.

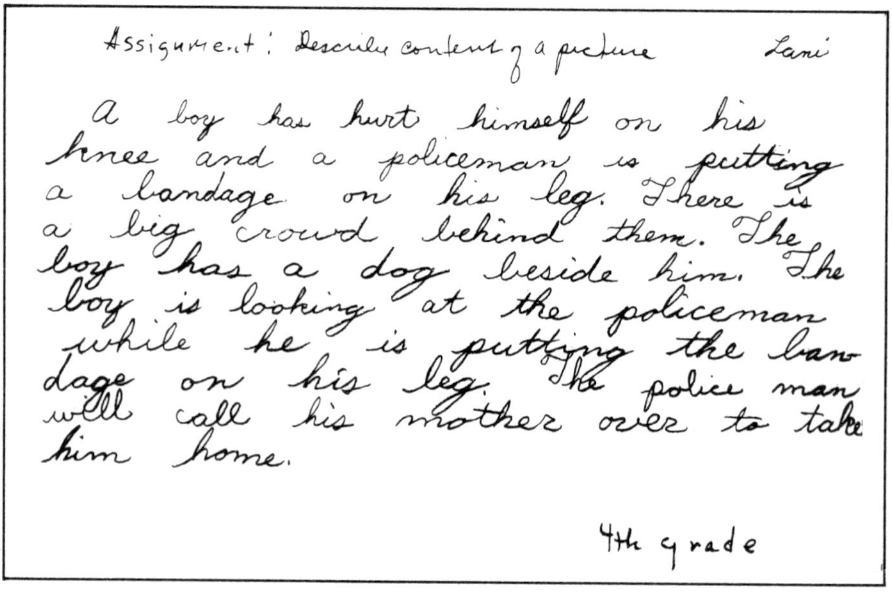

Assignment: Describe content of a picture   Lani

a boy has hurt himself on his
knee and a policeman is putting
a bandage on his leg. There is
a big crowd behind them. The
boy has a dog beside him. The
boy is looking at the policeman
while he is putting the bandage on his leg. The police man
will call his mother over to take
him home.

4th grade

Figure 5-4.

My name is Bob Kruger,I was born and raised in
Burlington WA.IlLove writting I intend to write many
more books.I have already written 2 books named <u>THE WAY</u>
<u>TO A MONSTERS HEART IS THROUGH HIS STOMACH</u>. and also
<u>ROVER AND THE CREATURE FROM THE CRACK</u>.I am now in the
6/th grade at WestView school in Burlington WA.and my
teacher is Mrs. Forbes.
     If you would like to own a copy of this book
please write to me at Bob Kruger 504 Galbreath Rd.
Burlington WA. 98233.

Figure 5–5.

Aside from the issue of writing quality, notice how the authors of these samples at the later grade levels are able to distance themselves psychologically from the topic and assume a reportive or objective stance. Melissa, on the other hand, for example, cannot resist personal comments on how she "likes" her cat.

Argumentative exposition, or, as it is sometimes called, persuasive writing is one of the more demanding of the modes of discourse or writing forms. Yet children in preschool years (as most parents know!) can be artful persuaders with oral language. Children in the primary grades can do likewise in their writing, although not nearly so elegantly as in their speech. Consider the examples in Figures 5–6 and 5–7.

Should a woman be president? 1st grade

yes a woman can be a president if you
don't think a woman can't be one then,
you well hafttofite with me and with
the presiden and hir husband so you
betr be cus I know they are rety O. k.
By Amy   March 10 1982

Figure 5–6.

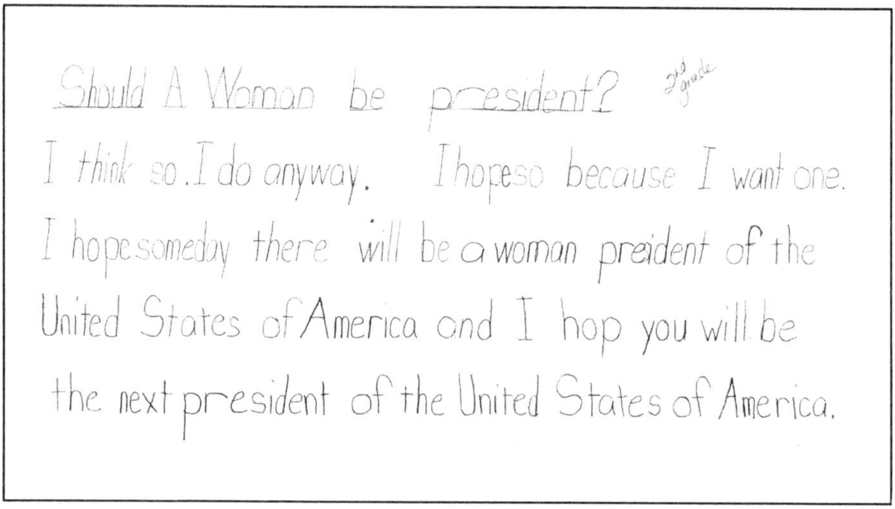

Should A Woman be president? *2nd grade*

I think so. I do anyway. I hope so because I want one.
I hope someday there will be a woman president of the
United States of America and I hop you will be
the next president of the United States of America.

Figure 5–7.

During the intermediate and middle school years, as objectivity, analytical skills, and logical organization improve, increased sophistication is to be expected in the persuasive mode of written expression. Consider the samples in Figures 5–8, 5–9, and 5–10.

Notice that the sample from the fourth grade lacks depth and is somewhat incoherent. However, it does assert a claim and does reach a conclusion. The two seventh-grade samples tackle more demanding topics and offer more elaboration. In both of these samples the thesis or claim is offered to the reader obliquely. The first sentence in neither paper really qualifies as a thesis assertion. In fact, the thesis assertion or claim is bound up directly in the conclusion in both samples. This is a persuasive technique, though probably too advanced for younger writers of argumentation. An initial thesis assertion sentence would have served as a more effective "advance organizer" than does an oblique or implied assertion.

Narrative writing differs from exposition primarily in the point of view assumed by the writer. In narrative writing the writer portrays events, people, objects, or situations from a personal viewpoint. The narrative form can thus appear in both fictional and nonfictional modes. And further, narrative and expository description or explanation overlap considerably. Perhaps even in one sense primary grade children do not write pure expository pieces, since their inability to distance themselves psychologically always forces a subjective writer stance on the writing. For example, consider the samples in Figures 5–11 and 5–12.

Notice how Kristie cannot resist the very subjective commentary on the results of the cookie baking! However, in the later grades, the narrative mode begins to take on its own distinctive character (see Figures 5–13 and 5–14).

CLAIM SENTENCE: Why we shoud go to school all week.

_____

_____

SUPPORT SENTENCES:

1. Because we will learn more._____

2. And we can play on the aquitment._____

3. And we wont get in trouble._____

4._____

5._____

6._____

7._____

CONCLUSION SENTENCE: We should go to school all week.

_____

_____

                                        4th grade
_____

_____

_____

_____

Figure 5–8.

```
                          LOTTERY


Many people think the Washington State lottery is fun.
It is to some people that win but most of the time you
don't win.

Most people that buy lottery tickets are poor.  They
spend their dollar on a ticket and they don't win.
But they keep on buying the tickets.

The poor people that buy the tickets are wasting their
money.  I think that they should make the lottery easier
to win.



                                    Mike

                                    Grade 7
```

Figure 5–9.

In the middle grades narrative is "fleshed out" and greater detail is provided. Not only is sentence structure more complex, but it also reflects the nature of the narrative mode more effectively. More extended and embedded relative clauses appear. Initial modifiers in sentences are chained to each other such that movement among different levels of abstraction is facilitated.

Creative writing in its more specialized use (as opposed to the valid general observation that all forms of writing require creative thought and expression) includes prose, poetry, and drama. Prose writing is that found typically in short stories and novels.

Poetry is a popular mode of writing for young children. It is one of the forms in which their products can reflect an honesty and a directness that enhance the quality of the writing beyond our expectations. Indeed, in the primary grades children are already producing poetry such as that shown in Figures 5–15 and 5–16. Poetry by intermediate and middle grade students reflects increased sophistication in both style and content.

Writing drama or play scripts is very demanding because it requires sustained application of the knowledge of critical elements of story grammar as well as a sense of timing. However, tied to creative drama activities, play writing serves as

CHOKEHOLD

The chokehold is a police technique that is taught in academies all over the United States. It is a technique used for self-defense.

The chokehold allows the officer to take control over a violent suspect without having to beat on him and break any bones. It is easy to do and to learn. It is a safe technique for the officer and it also works very effectively.

I think, that if it is used correctly it is o.k. for the policemen to use this technique but they should make <u>sure</u> that they know how to do it exactly or they can hurt people really seriously.

Allison

Grade 7

Figure 5–10.

Kristie
2nd grade

I help my Mommy bahe. cookies and we put chocolate chips in our cookies. They taste good.

(Notice the Final Statement!)

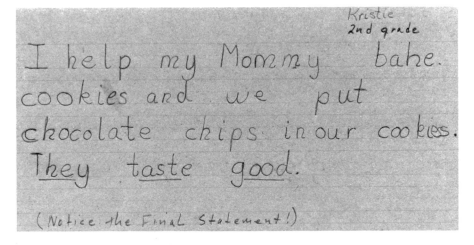

Figure 5–11.

Kristie

I help my Mommy ~~back~~ bake cookies and we put ~~choclit~~ chocolate chips in our cookies. ~~But~~ They taste good.

Figure 5–12.

an excellent activity. In addition, play writing efforts provide the student with firsthand involvement in a powerful set of concepts such as sequence, development, inference, organization, and the relationships of these concepts to theme, plot, and climax.

THE ELEMENTS OF WRITING

The elements of writing strand (in Table 5–1, p. 91) constitutes an important area of writing development. This strand focuses most directly on the final observable aspect of the written product—language structure. We shall treat three different categories within this strand—syntax (structure), uses of language, and logic of language.

Syntax (Structure)

Under syntax or structure there are two subcategories, sentence structure and paragraph structure. Within sentence structure, there are five areas of skills that students must acquire facility in—parts of speech, coordination, subordination, modification, and predication. This is what we normally refer to as grammar.

One day, as Danny Wilson was riding his bike,
walking Snoopy, his dog, he heard the ice-cream-man.
Danny was absolutely starving to death, so he
payed attention only to the sound of the
music. As Danny followed the loud jingle,
he hit a rock just at the right angle to
throw it up to hit his pants leg which
sent it towards the chain on his bike.
His pants got caught in the chain
which jolted the bike to stop and Danny
went flying off his bike into the ditch
and landed on his knees.

On the town which Danny lived was
very small, so whatever interesting thing
that happened made a big comotion, and
soon a crowd gathered around Danny
and Snoopy. They stood there for about
six minutes making stupid suggestions
to help him until finally a policeman
drove by, stopped, got out of his car, push
ed the crowd away (the crowd had about
13 people including Danny's best pals),
until he finally got to Danny.

After the policeman had got all his
first-aid out, he pulled up Danny's pant
leg to find a huge gash on his right
leg. By then the whole crowd had left
except for Danny's best pals. The policeman doctored the boy's leg until he
had it cleaned and bandaged. Then he
told Danny to hop in the squad and
make sure his dog wouldn't go to the
bathroom on the seat. Then he took
him home and when Danny's mother found out what happened, she
grounded not to get any ice-cream
whatsoever for 1 month.

Figure 5–13.

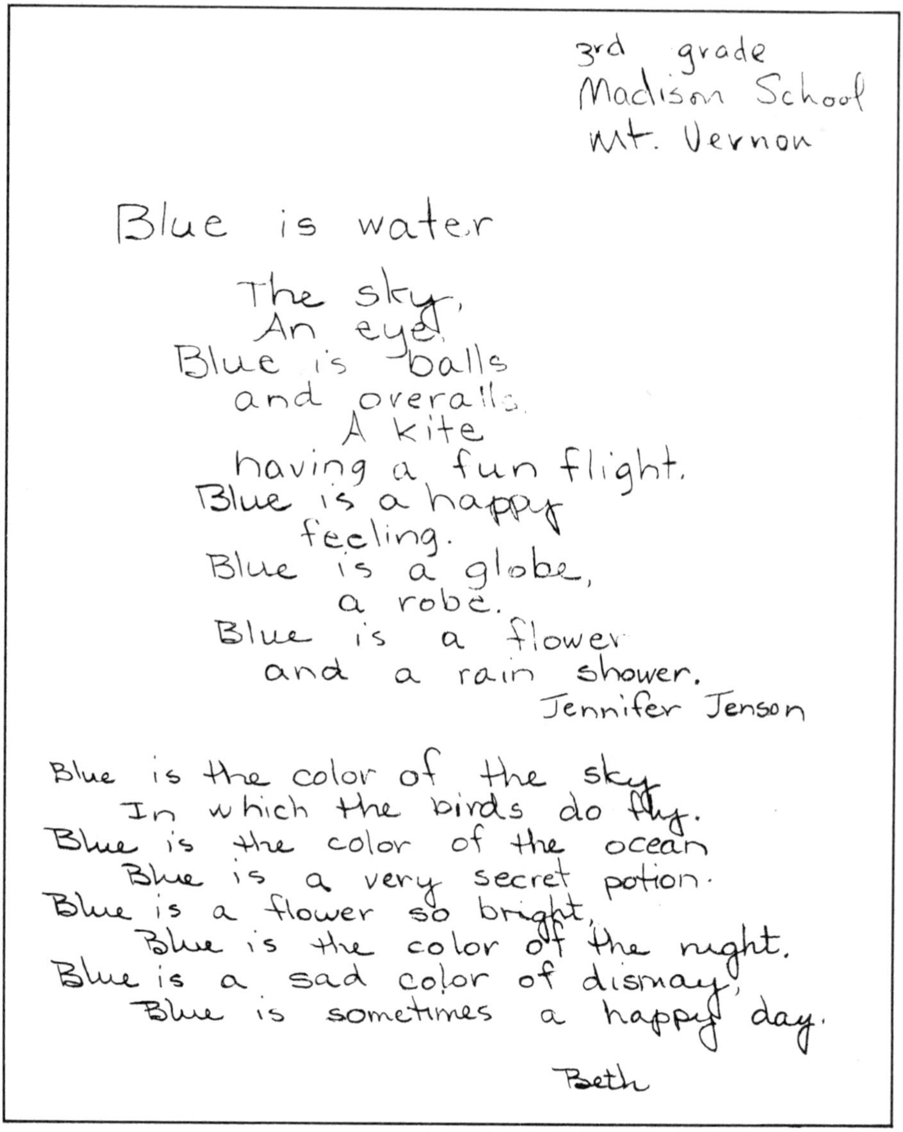

3rd grade
Madison School
Mt. Vernon

Blue is water

The sky,
An eye,
Blue is balls
and overalls.
A kite
having a fun flight.
Blue is a happy
feeling.
Blue is a globe,
a robe.
Blue is a flower
and a rain shower.

Jennifer Jenson

Blue is the color of the sky
In which the birds do fly.
Blue is the color of the ocean
Blue is a very secret potion.
Blue is a flower so bright,
Blue is the color of the night.
Blue is a sad color of dismay,
Blue is sometimes a happy day.

Beth

Figure 5-14.

Parts of speech   The parts of speech represent basic knowledge that the child has when entering school. The child uses nouns, verbs, adjectives, adverbs, and other parts of speech in their proper order and in semantic or definitional roles that are appropriate. The child has learned the nature and functions of the parts of speech through frequent verbalization. The amount of formal technical knowledge the child needs to learn about the parts of speech in the primary grades is limited.

The following general points should be made.

1. *Children in the first and second grades need not be taught formal termi-*

Figure 5–15.

Figure 5–16.

nology, that is, "verb," "noun," "adverb." Instead, activities in syntax should include reference to the labels "describing words" (adjectives, adverbs) and "naming words" (nouns and pronouns). Verbs present some problem. "Action words" do well for most, but the "to be" verbs (*am, are, is, was, were*), which are quite common, do not reflect action. Prepositions may be referred to as "location words," but we must remember that some adverbs also function that way, for example, "here."

2. *Grammar activities in the primary grades should focus primarily on sentence, clause, and phrase production rather than word or parts of speech analysis.*

3. *The terms for parts of speech should be introduced in the third grade* not *because children need to know them in order to speak or write properly but because our educational system incorporates basal language texts, a good deal of formalized grammar testing, and utilization of other curriculum guides and materials that either teach such terms or assume that the terms are being taught.*

4. *In the later grades, parts of speech should be taught from the standpoint of their structural features as much as from their unique or dominant semantic features.* For example, nouns do function as naming words. However, it is also useful to know that nouns are the only words that take a plural form and, along with pronouns, are the only words that show possession.

5. *Although more attention is given to the formal structural and semantic attributes of the parts of speech along with basic formal terminology in the later grades, fully two-thirds of instructional time in grammar then should focus on sentence production rather than sentence analysis.*

Coordination   Coordination in syntax is the act of joining words, phrases, or clauses, usually with *and, or,* or *but.* Later, coordination can be effected by use of '*for,*' '*however,*' and '*thus,*' among other words. Also, the semicolon allows for variety in style by serving in a coordinating role.

Predication   Predication involves two sets of grammatical constructs—verb phrases and predicate complements, such as direct objects (the boy hit *the ball*), predicate adjectives (the dress is *pretty*), and predicate nominatives (the girl is *the captain*). Object complements are also in this category (the team named Joe *the captain*).

Verb phrases are among the most difficult of the basic grammar concepts the young child must master. The English language includes an irregular verb set whose behaviors are "out of synch" with the regular verbs. This partially explains why typically first-graders tend to overextend the *ed* inflection, as in "He hurted his knee." Once again, however, the injunction against formalizing grammar unduly at this grade level becomes relevant. Children know how to use quite properly the bulk of the verb phrase constructs, in both speaking and writing, in their first-grade year. *What they need to be taught during their primary grades is not so much the explicit formal grammatical character of what they know, but the variety of application possibilities in sentence-building which they do not yet know.*

Modification Modification or description/elaboration/qualification in English can be performed by single words (adjectives and adverbs) or by phrases or clauses, as in "She is the girl *in the corner*" or "He is the one *that took the apple.*" The latter, clauses, and in particular relative clauses (those introduced by *who, which,* or *that*), are the syntactic units that are the most demanding of the writer.

Subordination Subordination in grammar is the act of reducing a clause (noun phrase plus verb phrase) to a dependent status not standing alone as a sentence) by introducing it with a subordinate conjunction (*although, since, because, if*). For example: "*Since the children worked hard,* they were given the afternoon off" or "The team lost *because they had not practiced enough.*"

The ability to utilize subordination effectively is critical to effective writing. It is also one of the most demanding sentence-building skills in writing, and thus is not mastered until the later grades. Even second-graders, for example, use *because* as a *coordinate* conjunction rather than a subordinate conjunction indicating a cause-effect relationship.

Uses of Language

There are only two basic uses to which language may be put in either speaking or writing. We either assert something about someone or something, or we use language for nonassertive purposes by questioning or exclaiming or directing someone to do something. We can classify sentences and utterances into these two broad domains, and, further, we can categorize whole pieces of discourse, written and spoken, in the same way.

Nonassertive language uses Although there are three subcategories of nonassertive language use, exclaiming, as a type, is relegated largely to single sentences or utterances. The other two, inquiring/questioning and directing, can appear as paragraphs or compositions in writing. For example, paragraphs of inquiry and paragraphs providing directions about how to assemble something, play something, or get to a location are all quite possible and are fairly common. However, most paragraphs of inquiry are either embedded within a longer composition which asserts a thesis, or they are rhetorical in character and actually imply an assertion. For practical purposes, nearly all writing falls into the assertive category.

Assertive language uses There are three major assertive uses of language that students must master in order to be effective writers—describing, explaining, and proposing or arguing something.

Description tends to be more objective than explanation. To describe simply means to elaborate the features or aspects of an object, event, or idea. However, to explain the same thing implies a commitment to offer a reasonably substantive presentation of underlying causal factors or a logical accounting for the processes or operations involved.

Since the differences between description and explanation can be rather subtle, explanation seldom appears in the early primary grades. However, by the intermediate grades, the differences between these two assertive language uses need to be taught.

Argumentation, as a language use, is perhaps the most elegant of the assertive category. And it, too, should be introduced early, but with little anticipation of effective implementation until the intermediate and middle school years.

The Logic of Language Use

One of the most important writing skills students must master is not only that of writing individual sentences well but that of knowing how to put well-written individual sentences into a composition so that the intersentence relationships are appropriate. In effect, they must learn to write so that one sentence reasonably and logically follows from preceding ones and can itself serve as a vehicle to the sentences that follow.

Two major skills here are important—sequence and unity/coherence. The two are closely related to each other as well as to other skills that need to be elaborated individually in the later grades, for example, conciseness and use of effective transitional devices and techniques. These more technical and/or sophisticated rhetorical skills can all be subsumed under our two general subcategories for purposes of instruction in the elementary grades.

Ability at sequencing ideas, events, and happenings properly is a critical writing skill with direct ties to other literacy measures such as reading comprehension. Learners need ample instruction in and practice with applying this rhetorical skill.

The ability to develop a topic in a logical fashion is connected to the rhetorical skill of sequencing. However, logical development entails more than simply ordering items in proper array. Also involved in logical development are decisions such as: What information should I include or leave out? How much elaboration should I give to which events or ideas? How should I state my conclusions? These more demanding skills are acquired over the later years.

Skill in composing with effective logical development is not an end goal or terminal objective that is conclusively reached at a particular time. Instead, it is an ability in writing that evolves and becomes more sophisticated and subtle as the writer matures and extends his range of syntactic and semantic options.

Unity or coherence refers to the ''sticking or holding together'' of the total composition, whether it be an essay, a paragraph, or even a sentence, for either a sentence has internal coherence or it does not. Writing that reflects coherence or unity is well sequenced and has logical development. However, it has more as well. It has carefully chosen descriptors and a balance of grammatical constructions rather than overuse of any one sentence pattern. It reads as if leaving out one word or sentence might destroy it.

THE IMPINGING FACTORS
OF CIRCUMSTANCE

"The impinging factors of circumstance" include a variety of "things" that impose themselves upon the writer, often things the writer has little say in determining. For example, subjects or topics for writing are often assigned by teachers, so the student must deal with what is given. Audience, setting, subject, and purpose are similar in that respect. Nevertheless, though they are not as tangible as skills such as grammar application skills, they turn out to be critical factors when the reader decides whether to read the writing, and, if he does decide to read it, what sort of posture he will take toward the writer. The student must learn that a crucial part of writing is doing it in a way that develops a sympathetic audience. Remember—no audience, no communication!

Audience

The student must learn to apply writing skills that address the three different senses of audience discussed earlier—self, personal or known you, and the unknown you. Each audience sense creates a little more psychological distance between the writer and reader as one moves away from the self as audience.

Setting

When we refer to stories, the setting is the place and time of the sequence of events or plot that is elaborated. In our composition curriculum framework, however, setting refers to the condition or situation within which the writing occurs. This setting can be very personal or intimate, informal, formal, or, in extreme cases, ceremonial. Examples of the latter are marriage ceremonies or court behavior rituals during trials. In ceremonial settings, in fact, most of the information conveyed is subsurface. That is, what is said in a marriage ceremony, for example, is less tied to the meaning of the words themselves than to their traditional *symbolical* significance.

In highly formal settings, on the other hand, the precise meaning of every word is important. And, in writing, formal settings require extreme care in use of all the presentational amenities as well as the elements of writing.

When we write in informal settings, our style can be a little more relaxed. We can tolerate occasional mechanical errors. We are usually communicating with friends, for example, by letter, and they are usually tolerant of our minor grammatical infractions. They are more concerned about the "what" of our writing.

The intimate or highly personal setting is such that a few scrawled notes or signs often suffice since only we as writers read what is produced or only the very closest of friends who know us quite well will read it.

Notice the close relationship between senses of audience and setting. Self-as-

Audience is usually tied to the intimate or highly personal setting, while the Unknown You audience is typically associated with a Formal or Ceremonial Setting.

Students need to be in composition programs which help them discover these sorts of important relationships between rhetorical concepts.

Subject

The subjects or topics about which we write can vary considerably from animate to inanimate; personal to nonpersonal; abstract to specific; and abstract to concrete. In the early primary grades, topics should focus on concrete, personal and animate categories, with a gradual incorporation of the other subject types as the learner moves to the later elementary grades.

Purpose

There are a number of purposes for writing: to inform, to describe, to explain, to inquire, to direct, to persuade, and to enjoy.

Writing to inform, to describe, and to explain we shall collapse into the general category of Reportive Writing for the primary grades. Writing to inquire and to direct will remain as separate though smaller categories. Writing to persuade will serve as a separate category as, too, will writing to enjoy.

Notice again the relationships which hold within our composition framework. Reportive, Inquiry, and Directive purposes are usually written in the expository mode, Persuasive purposes by the argumentative expository mode, and writing to enjoy through the creative mode. Both writing to entertain and writing to report can also overlap with the narrative mode.

What the composition curriculum framework does is provide us with an overview of the components instrumental to the development of an effective writer. Failure to attend to and seriously incorporate all of the presentational amenities, elements of writing, and impinging factors of circumstance leaves the writer in the situation of trying to learn to write without a complete picture of what it is that constitutes quality composition. In addition, without a comprehensive approach to the tasks of writing instruction, the learner is much more likely to elevate particular skills or concepts to positions of importance that are inappropriate.

In the next chapter we shall consider activities, techniques, and strategies that assist the classroom teacher in implementing writing instruction according to the various features of the composition curriculum framework.

NOTES

1. R. Hodges, *Learning to Spell* (Urbana, Ill.: NCTE/ERIC, 1981).

Writing Activities
and Teaching Ideas
for Grades 1 Through 8

chapter
6

The primary purpose of this chapter is to provide an array of suggested techniques and activities of practical teaching value. However, it is important that the teacher keep in mind a number of points.

1. These activities and techniques are intended to do two things. First, they should illustrate the kind or type of activity or technique that may appropriately fit in the composition curriculum framework. Second, they can serve as models or samples that teachers can use to develop further materials of their own for teaching or to use as guides for the selection of commercially developed materials.

2. The order of presentation and the general sequencing of these ideas are *not* intended to suggest that they should be taught in a specific manner throughout the grades or within any given grade. That is, the presentational amenities are not intended necessarily to be taught prior to the elements of writing. Within each of the subcategories, however, there is a *general* ordering by level of complexity in the activities.

3. Many of the activities—perhaps even most—overlap with others in terms of the skills and concepts taught. This suggests again that most writing skills are most effectively taught in an integrated fashion. For example, when children engage in sentence-combining activity, they are also addressing matters such as style and the uses and logic of language. Children developing skills in the use and application of the expository modes are also learning logical skills.

4. The composition curriculum framework is primarily concerned with laying out the processes, skills, and concepts of writing. And, although many of the various ideas within the framework provide suggestions for the writing process— preparing for the writing, writing follow-up, setting the stage for writing, and

providing an open and encouraging writing environment—one cannot overemphasize the fact that it is the classroom teacher who determines the success or failure of the composition program by creating an environment for writing so that the various skills and concepts of composition can be effectively taught.

PRESENTATIONAL AMENITIES

Recall that the primary role of the presentational amenities is supportive. They do not, on the whole, enter into the writing act but rather "decorate" the result so it is acceptable in appearance. Since many of these amenities tend to be somewhat mechanical in nature, it is a challenge for the teacher to come up with creative and unique ways to teach them. We shall consider various samples to explore in the three subcategories of mechanics, style, and modes of discourse.

Mechanics

HANDWRITING

Although there is certainly satisfaction to be derived from attractive handwriting, our concern should be first and foremost with developing writers who write legibly and comfortably.

In an overall approach to handwriting instruction there are a few "do's and don'ts" to keep in mind:

1. Remember, even in early stages, copying letters appears to be more helpful than tracing activities.
2. Do not worry about using oversized writing instruments. Regular pencils are fine.
3. Provide practice daily but for short periods. Avoid fatigue and boredom.
4. Have children practice forming real letters rather than abstract shapes such as semicircles.
5. Incorporate art and drawing activities heavily in the early stages of the handwriting program.

All programs need activities and skill-building opportunitites in a few important areas. Following are samples that may be used to reinforce the ongoing handwriting program.

MAKING LETTERS, WORDS, AND SENTENCES

Materials Toothpicks, pieces of yarn or heavy string of various lengths, small beans, circles, angles, horseshoe-shaped cardboard pieces that have been cut out with scissors.

Directions Provide ample supplies of the materials. Print several lowercase manuscript letters on the board or place letter models in the chalk tray. Ask the children to make their own copies of the letters by using their materials. Move around the room and respond to each child's efforts. Discuss with the students how curves, straight lines, and angles are important in writing.

Eventually give them words to copy and later short sentences.

FINGERPAINTING

Materials Paper, fingerpaints, paper towels, and damp cloths for cleanup.

Directions Provide children with ample supplies and a comfortable work area. Initially, have them copy objects such as a clock face, a simple building, a human figure. Subjects such as these provide practice in most of the line configurations and movements needed in handwriting.

Later ask them to copy letters, words, and short sentences.

WRITING LOOP LETTERS

Materials Pencil and paper.

Directions (1) Have children copy a tongue twister with loop letters, for example, "Peter Piper picked a peck of pickled peppers." (2) Write a word with loop letters on the board and ask children to think of as many words as they can that contain the letters and write them down. (3) Ask children to think of words that contain both upper-loop (*p*'s, for example) and lower-loop (*g*'s or *f*'s, for example) letters, and write them down (*foal* and *goof,* for example).

WRITING THE MID-LETTERS (d, t, a, c, e, etc.)

Materials Pencil and paper.

Directions (1) Write a word phrase with alliteration (same beginning letters in each) and ask the students to copy it. For example, "Ten Tall Turtles" or "Cute Cuddly Cats" or "Many Mad Men." (2) Ask the students to make up their own alliterative phrases and write them down. They can compare phrases with each other. The students may also be paired up, with each pair producing phrases.

Once the child has mastered the basic handwriting skills, additional instruction should take place largely within the context of the total writing program, with meaningful communication as an organizing principle for the selection and design of handwriting activities.

Basic References on Handwriting

ANDERSON, D. W. *What Research Says to the Teacher: Teaching Handwriting.* Washington, D.C.: National Education Association, 1968.

ASKOV, E.: OTTO, W.: and ASKOV, W. "A Decade of Research in Handwriting: Progress and Prospect." *Journal of Educational Research,* 64 (1970): 99–111.

HORN, T. D., ed. *Research on Handwriting and Spelling.* Urbana, Ill.: National Council of Teachers of English, 1966.

STEWIG, J. *Exploring Language With Children.* Columbus, Ohio: Chas. E. Merrill, 1974.

FREEMAN, F. "On Italic Handwriting." *Elementary School Journal,* 60 (February 1960): 258–64.

SPELLING

In most elementary schools, instruction in spelling is based upon some commercially published basal program. And, although these differ in philosophy and approach, there are a couple of things that all programs and spelling authorities probably agree upon. One is that children must develop an ability to associate the important sounds of words with the various letters and letter combinations in our language that can represent those sounds. A second is that, although there are a number of idiosyncratic characteristics of our spelling system, there are also a number of generalizations we can make that help us become better spellers. Helping students learn and apply those generalizations is important. Many also suggest need for practice in learning to spell certain "demons," or words that consistently cause spelling problems. There are yet others who propose that most spelling is learned within the larger arena of writing, where linguistic context and need for communication provide incentives for correct spelling not found in other approaches.

Following are activities categorized in such a way that they should serve as models or samples of types that can fit into most spelling programs:

EXPLORING SOUND-LETTER RELATIONSHIPS: PRIMARY GRADES

Spelling Cards

Materials Cards that have been made by either pasting on pictures from old magazines or with drawings in felt-tip pen style and with the name of the object under the picture. The cards should be in sets of four or five with three out of four or four out of five having the same initial letters and sounds or some internal vowels and letters in common. For example, *pie, pen, pig* and *car* might be in one set; *look, cook, took* and *joke* in another.

Directions Children are asked to select the one card that doesn't fit and tell why. This can also be a small group or paired activity. Also, the class can be divided into teams and contests held to see who can spot the out-of-place card first. The complexity can be increased or decreased by altering the number of cards and by choosing different objects or events and associated words.

Rhyming Games

Materials   None.

Directions   Children are asked to think of a word that rhymes with another, then provide a definition that will help others guess the word. For example, "I am thinking of a word that rhymes with cat, and you use it in baseball games" (bat). A variation is for you to provide words and ask children to list as many words as they can that rhyme with the given word.

INFERRING GENERALIZATIONS: INTERMEDIATE AND MIDDLE SCHOOL GRADES

Materials   None.

Directions   List a series of words on the board whose spellings are the result of the application of a spelling generalization. Ask the children to guess why a similar word is sounded differently; for example, an activity to help children recognize the role of the silent final *e* in making the internal vowel long. Consider:

(1) *take,*
(2) *cake,*
(3) *make,*
(4) *lake,*
(5) *Kate,*
   but
(6) *cat.* How are 1 and 6 alike? How different? What is different about the spelling of *cat*? What can we say about words with internal vowels that end with silent *e*?

Word Building

Spelling clusters such as prefixes, suffixes, and root words represent an important opportunity to relate spelling to word meaning. Further, they represent an opportunity to relate spelling to vocabulary development. Therefore, word-building activities deserve a prominent place in any spelling program.

WORD SCRAMBLES

Materials   Several sets of cardboard squares, each with a different letter of the alphabet printed or drawn on it.

Directions   There are a variety of spelling games that can be done with these materials. They can be arranged in piles with varying numbers of letters that can be used to spell a variety of words. Children, given a pile, can be asked to create as many words as they can from the pile, writing them down as they go along.

Another variation is to place the letters face down and scrambled. Students can then be asked to draw a set number of cards and see who can spell the most words with the cards drawn.

Other variations include dealing the cards out, as in a card game, with the winner being the child who spells the most words.

Several letters can be given to groups of students—4 to 5 per group—with the challenge being to spell the most words possible within each group.

Materials   Cards similar to those used in the previous activity. However, rather than letters, root words, prefixes, and suffixes are printed on them.

Directions   Similar to those for word scrambles. Place appropriate prefixes, (*un-*, *non-*) with possible root words in a group. However, also include some combinations that won't work so the student must make the legitimate connections.

Materials   Make "word squares" of various types, for example:

C	R	E
A	D	T
I	M	O

Build a collection of cards of varying complexity (that is, arrays of 9 squares, 12 squares, 16 squares), distribute them to students, and ask them to create as many words as they can (the same letter can be used more than once if desired).

Word square puzzles can be made on duplicating masters with students asked to circle words vertically, horizontally, or diagonally. For example:

I	M	X	O	O
F	A	S	T	F
N	M	E	A	Y
K	B	E	R	T
R	L	N	Q	P

Again, complexity can be increased or decreased as desired.

Spelling is one of the most important of the presentational amenities, so its role must be assured. However, as with so many other skills in this strand, spelling needs to be taught, when possible, in linguistically meaningful contexts. There should be interest and motivation underlying all spelling activities. And the impact of proper spelling on the total written product needs to be stressed rather than spelling for its own sake.

Basic Spelling References

ALLRED, R. A. *Spelling: The Application of Research Findings.* Washington, D.C.: National Education Association, 1977.
FRITH, U., ed. *Cognitive Processes in Spelling.* London: Academic Press, 1980.
HODGES, R. E. *Learning to Spell.* Urbana, Ill.: NCTE/ERIC, 1981.
HENDERSON, E. H., and BEERS, J. W., eds. *Developmental and Cognitive Aspects of Learning to Spell: A Reflection of Word Knowledge.* Newark, Del.: International Reading Association, 1980.
MULAC, M. E. *Educational Games for Fun.* New York: Harper & Row Publishers, 1971.

PUNCTUATION AND CAPITALIZATION

Punctuation and capitalization are important for the writer to master. They are critical to the reader who has not the benefit of voice inflection and gesture or facial expression to denote the message in appropriate places.

The teaching of punctuation marks, commas, and quotation marks especially occurs over the years, with only basic attention to them in the primary grades. A general grade-level guide for teaching punctuation marks in the early grades follows:

In the first grade introduce:

use of the period
use of the question mark
use of the comma in these contexts:
    between day of month and year
    between city and state
    after the salutation in a friendly letter
    after letter closing
use of the apostrophe in contractions and possessives
use of quotation marks in dialogue situations

In the second and third grade, teach all of the above, plus:

extend teaching of comma use to separation of words in a series, direct address, and selected coordinate clause separations

> use of the apostrophe
> limited use of the colon and hyphen
> use of the exclamation mark

For capitalization instruction, the following is appropriate:
In the first grade, teach capitalization of:

> first word of sentence
> first and last names
> name of street
> the pronoun *I*
> name of city and school
> names of days and months
> important words in titles
> abbreviations
> initials

In the second and third grades, add all other capitalization skills, including:

> poetry lines
> names of organizations and societies
> outline topic words
> titles of ranks

Some general observations on teaching these skills:

> Tie instruction to teaching of proofreading and revision skills when possible.
>
> For variety, use oral dictation drills where you slightly exaggerate the voice inflection to emphasize the relationship of pitch and pause in speech to punctuation in writing.
>
> Keep a variety of practice sheets and materials on hand to be used spontaneously, permitting you to "fill in" time between scheduled activities with maximally useful instruction and practice.
>
> Design and use a monitoring chart or checkoff list for each pupil to assist in maintaining a skill development record.
>
> Do not allow instruction in these skills to offset the importance of the other composition skills: These are the building blocks; they are the structure.

Following are a variety of activities and ideas for fitting punctuation and capitalization skill instruction into the writing program.

ORAL DICTATION ACTIVITIES

Materials   Separate sets of cards for each child showing punctuation marks.

Directions   Read sentences to the students with exaggerated voice inflection and pauses to provide cues to the placement of the correct punctuation. The students

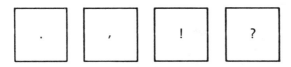

should hold up the appropriate card to identify the punctuation mark needed. This can be conducted as a game with scores given to individual students, sides of the room, or individual groups competing against each other.

Materials Ditto handouts showing unpunctuated sentences.

Directions Read sentences aloud to the students with exaggerated voice inflection while they punctuate the corresponding sentences on handouts. Then have the students compare their work to see whether they agree or disagree.

Another version is to have the students work in pairs, with one assigned the reading responsibility and the other the punctuation task. The act of reading with proper inflection helps the reader make the necessary connections between the rhythm of the language and punctuation.

Materials None.

Directions Write a single sentence on the board with punctuation and/or capitalization errors. Ask children to spot the error(s) and discuss as a class. There is no writing in this activity, but, again, it enables students to begin to see the ties between oral and written punctuation.

PUNCTUATION/CAPITALIZATION GAMES

Intermediate and Middle School Grades

Materials Maintain in your files duplicating masters and ditto handouts of sentences in lists, sentences in paragraphs, and paragraphs in sequence as compositions, all of which have deliberate punctuation and capitalization errors. These may be categorized according to theme (for example, holidays, events, scenes, places). Further, they may be categorized according to error type or according to some other system.

Divide the class in half or into small groups. Have each student correct errors on his or her handout. You may have contests in which the winning side is determined by speed of *correct* completion. Or you may determine the winners by number of errors corrected or left uncorrected.

Students can also be asked to create sentences or paragraphs of their own with errors for correction. These can be exchanged and utilized in setting up class teams for competition.

In activities of this sort keep in mind that context and meaning are important for the student to see something worthwhile in the activity.

Basic References on Punctuation and Capitalization

BURNS, P. C., and BASSETT, R. *Language Arts Activities for Elementary Schools.* Boston: Houghton Mifflin, 1982.

HENNINGS, D. G. *Communication in Action: Teaching the Language Arts, 2nd ed.* Boston: Houghton Mifflin, 1982.

MOFFETT, J., and WAGNER, B. *Student-Centered Language Arts and Reading, K–13.* Boston: Houghton Mifflin, 1983.

PETTY, W.; PETTY, D.; and BECKING, M. *Experiences in Language: Tools and Techniques for Language Arts Methods.* Boston: Allyn & Bacon, Inc., 1981.

VAIL, N., and PAPENFUSS, J. *Daily Oral Language.* Racine, WI: D. O. L. Publications, 1981.

Style

The concept of writer's style is quite complex, for it requires not only mastery of individual skills and concepts in writing but also knowledge of how most effectively they can be combined in order to both reflect the content of the message and the posture of the writer in the writing act.

This is a facility that continually evolves and becomes increasingly sophisticated as the writer matures. During the primary grades, major focus needs to be on those aspects of the language that are instructionally accessible. The child in these grades can deal only with very basic aspects of usage, vocabulary, and structural choices within sentences. However, an understanding that these factors are closely allied to the purpose and form of the writing and the audience for which the writing is intended comes in the later grades.

Following are selected activities or ideas for teaching the rudiments of style.

WORD CHOICE

Primary Grades

Materials   Handouts with short paragraphs and word choice options such as the following:

The _____ girl found a _____ in the street. She
      (tiny, huge, mean, little)   (dog, puppy, animal)

_____ away from it at first. Then she went back to _____
(ran, walked, skipped)   (look, stare, see)

again because she was _____ .
                        (sorry, sad, happy)

Directions   Ask the students to choose one of the option words for each blank space. Then have them rewrite the paragraph using their word choices. Have the students read their papers aloud in class and discuss the differences in meaning and how the words we choose affect our reactions to the writing.

A shorter version of the activity is to simply provide single sentences with only one or two word choices available. A more advanced version is to provide only words that are synonyms, but with significantly different connotations. For example: "The man was (ugly, hideous, not handsome)." "The lady was (fat, plump, fairly large)." "The girl (looked, stared, glared) at the boy."

In activities such as these, students begin to learn that the meaning of a written passage reflects the writer's point of view.

Playing with Nonsense Words

Materials   Handouts or a transparency on an overhead projector with short paragraphs utilizing nonsense words. For example: "Ellen got out of bed one morning and decided to ride her *ZUNI* to school. After breakfast, she put her books in the basket on the *ZUNI*. Then she rode her *ZUNI* to school."

Directions   Ask the students to guess what a "ZUNI" is after reading the paragraph together. Ask them to tell how they know. What were some words or sentences that helped?

Students learn that the writer's choice of content and the reader's past experience both play an important role in composition.

LOOKING AT DIALECTS

Intermediate and Middle Grades

Materials   Records or tapes of people (preferably peer-group students) reading a story or narrative passage. The reader should be from a region of the country with a distinctly different dialect. Also have one or more tape recorders and blank tapes available.

Directions   Have the students tape their own voices reading stories or passages similar to those on tape. Play the tape of the dialect-different reader interspersed with a tape of one or more of your students. Ask students to note the differences in how the voices sound. If there are any vocabulary differences, ask them to note those as well. Talk about how people in different parts of the country use language differently and that one way of talking is not necessarily better or worse than another (within the context of the dialect differences that exist).

Another version of this activity that requires some planning and is best as a longer-range project is as follows. Have students each read a brief passage or story and tape it. Type up copies of the story. Find out if any of your students have friends or relatives in schools in other parts of the country—look particularly for those where there is likely to be a dialect difference, for example, New England vs. Deep South, rural vs. urban. Obtain the address of the school of interest. Have the students compose a letter telling about their project, and then you prepare an introductory letter for the teacher. Ask the students in the other part of the country to please read the story you are enclosing onto tape and mail it back. This tape exchange project can grow each year.

In activities such as these students learn to appreciate differences in language usage and expression as natural and attractive in language. Further, they become personally involved as actual subjects demonstrating some of those language usage differences. Most important, they begin to see how "style" or presentation in language—both oral and written—is shaped by a wide range of factors, including our dialect.

Oral usage   Note the oral dictation activities in the previous section on production and capitalization. The same format and materials can be used in this section by simply changing the error or inappropriate language focus to usage areas, such as subject-verb agreement, pronoun case and/or pronoun-antecedent agreement, and so on.

Recall in the research and theory review that oral usage is intricately bound to the communication context. And establishing a variety of these contexts for students is likely to be more productive than any combination of language drills in isolation.

Selected References on Style

EASTON, L., and KLEIN, M. *Expressways*. Oklahoma City: The Economy Co., 1984.

JENSEN, J., and PETTY, W. T. *Developing Children's Language*. Boston: Allyn & Bacon, 1980.

MCCRACKEN, M., and MCCRACKEN, R. *Reading, Writing and Language: A Practical Guide for Primary Teachers*. Winnipeg: Penguin Publishers, 1979.

MOFFETT, J., and WAGNER, B. *Student-Centered Language Arts and Reading, K–12*. Boston: Houghton Mifflin, 1983.

VAIL, N., and PAPENFUSS, J. *Daily Oral Language*. Racine, Wisc.: D. O. L. Publications, 1981.

Modes of Discourse (Writing Forms)

Students in the elementary grades should be provided opportunities to write in all three of the critical modes of written discourse—expository, narrative, and creative. Further, they should be writing in each of the subcategories addressed within each mode. For expository writing, they should have experience writing reportive (descriptive, explanatory, or informative) compositions and argumentative or persuasive ones as well.

Narrative writing activities should include narration in both nonfiction and fiction contexts. Creative writing opportunities should include prose, poetry, and drama writing.

Ideas for Narrative Writing
in the Primary Grades

The following suggestions draw heavily upon the oral language base of the child. Additional activities in a solid composition program should also incorporate oral language with the teaching of narrative writing.

Taping stories   The cassette tape recorder is a particularly powerful tool for the primary grades, for it enables children to compose stories orally or narrative texts even prior to being able to write or with greater elaboration potential than they can exhibit in early writing development stages. Among the various options available for incorporating the cassette tape recorder into the writing program are:

> Children compose stories orally in a quiet corner. The tapes are then sent to children in later grades where they are transcribed and returned in written form.
>
> Children are provided a picture of an action scene or event, for example, an approaching accident between two vehicles at an intersection. The child acts as an on-the-scene radio commentator describing in his own words what is occurring. This activity can be used in a variety of settings where the narrator tapes a description of a play, a ball game, a fight, or similar event.
>
> Children take small cassette tape recorders with them on a field trip (perhaps to an arboretum, for example). They make "oral notes" or observations about the things they see. When they return to the school, they listen to their notes as "memory joggers" and then write brief narratives describing their experiences.
>
> Children are provided with partly dictated stories on tapes. They listen to the stories and then complete them on tape. (The teacher can control the complexity easily here by deciding how much of the story framework to provide.) These tapes can be transcribed later if desired.

Picture narrating   Provide children with picture sequences, for example, comic strips with the dialogue balloons. Ask children to write about what they think is happening. They can later read their narratives aloud while referring to the pictures. Of course, photographs or slides may also be used instead of comic strips in picture narrating.

Narrative writing within the fictional modes   Have children make up a character who might appear in a story or play. (Ask early primary grade children to draw a picture of a "weird" character.) Ask them to write descriptions of their character so that readers will know not only what he looks like but also what kind of person he is—mean or kind, cowardly or brave.

> Describe to students the plot for a ghost story you would like to write. You need to have a beginning written that describes an old castle in the mountains in a spooky fashion.
>
> Have the students read a story (or read it to them). Ask them to think of a character not in the story that they might make up to be put into the story. Ask them to write a description of that character (an extension would be to ask them also where the character should be placed in the story).

Ideas for Narrative Writing
in the Upper Elementary
and Middle School Grades

As students reach the later grades, instruction should move on two fronts. First, activities and experiences such as those elaborated earlier for young children should be continued, expanded, developed into major instructional units and approaches. Journal writing, use of the cassette tape recorder and notebooks for recording field-based data from interviews, and other similar activities provide important opportunities for narrative writing instruction. Further, narrative writing should be taught in the context of creative writing as well. Character development and setting are focal points of narration in the fictional mode.

A second area of importance for the writer of narration, however, is that of the structure of sentences and paragraphs in the narrative mode. The language of narration is unique, and the developing writer must grasp that uniqueness and apply it. For example, sentences in narrative writing, more than any other type, reflect patterns of abstraction-level movement both within and across paragraphs. These patterns can serve as structural models for students to use in elaborating the data they have accumulated in their notebooks or on field trips.

Following is a general sequence of activities that can help intermediate and middle school students develop essential skills in recognizing and applying these structural patterns of narrative writing.*

Teaching two kinds of sentences   Discuss the following ideas with students, using handouts and, if possible, an overhead projector.

Telling sentences can be divided into two groups. One kind of telling sentence is the particular, or singular, kind. It says something about an individual person, fact, or idea. Here are some examples of particular or singular statements:

1. Joe lives on the hill.
2. Fred is my friend.
3. The sun was shining this morning.

A second kind of telling sentence is the generalization. It says something about a larger number of people, things, or ideas and what they do or have in common as a group. Here are some examples of generalizations: (1) All of the fans like football. (2) Many girls race motorcycles. (3) Some of my friends are in high school.

Notice that words like *all of, many,* and *some of* can serve as clues that a telling sentence is a generalization. Sometimes, however, generalizations do not

---

*Selected activities in the following are from M. Klein, "One Technique for Teaching Narrative Writing," *North Carolina English Teacher* (Summer 1981), 7–17. Reprinted by permission.

have specific quantity terms in them. For example: (1) People are funny. (2) Horses tend to bite. (3) Babies often cry. The plural noun can be a clue in generalizations like these.

The most difficult generalization to recognize might be the kind that has a singular noun subject but tells something that the subject does repeatedly or continu- . ously. For example: (1) The sun shines daily. [Here the word *daily* is a useful clue.] (2) Joe always smiles. [*Always* is a good clue in this generalization.] (3) She races motorcycles.

In generalization 3, we are talking about only one person but something she likes doing or does often. In other words, the sentence is a generalization because it refers to continuous behavior.

Ask students to see if they can tell singular statements from generalizations. Ask them to put a *G* in front of each generalization and an *S* in front of each singular statement among the following:

1. The red motorcycle is fun to ride.
2. Motorcycles are fun to ride.
3. A fool and his money are soon parted.
4. A few of the sentences are difficult.

Tell why each is a generalization or a particular or singular statement.

Have students make up singular statements and generalizations. Include some generalizations with quantity terms (*all, most*) and some without them. Compare and discuss these in small groups.

A useful and interesting supplementary activity is one using abstraction ladders. For example, below are ladders with terms on the rungs. As one goes up the ladder, terms become more specific.

1.
| 1983 Suzuki 1100 |
| Suzuki 1100 |
| 1100 Street Bike |
| Street Bike |
| Motorcycle |

2.
| Bessie |
| Cow |
| Livestock |
| Animal |

Fill in the rungs on the following ladder with appropriate terms:

The complexity of the task can be varied by altering the number of rungs and by varying the placement of the given term or terms on particular rungs.

The same technique can be used with sentences rather than individual terms placed on rungs. For example,

| The old '47 Ford pickup was stuck in the ditch near the cornfield. |
| The old pickup was stuck in the ditch. |
| The old pickup was stuck. |
| The pickup was stuck. |

Narrative paragraph patterns   Introduce the following four structural paragraph patterns for narrative writing to students. The system of indenting is designed to indicate whether a given sentence is more specific or less abstract than the previous one or ones.

#1 Generalization (Topic Sentence)
    Particular Statement
        Particular Statement
Generalization   Particular Statement   Particular Statement

Here is a paragraph using the #1 paragraph pattern:

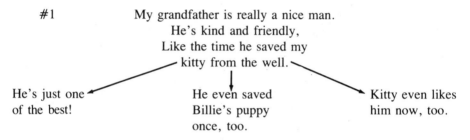

#1   My grandfather is really a nice man.
       He's kind and friendly,
       Like the time he saved my
       kitty from the well.

He's just one   He even saved   Kitty even likes
of the best!   Billie's puppy   him now, too.
       once, too.

Notice that the writer has a choice of three different kinds of sentences to use in ending the paragraph.

Following is another paragraph using this pattern but on a different subject:

#1 Kenny Roberts is an excellent motorcycle racer.
    He has won several races in this country.
      He has won at flat track and at TT.
        This past spring he won the European
        Grand Prix of Motorcycling.

He is an all-   He even won the Daytona   I wouldn't be
around good   Open several times.   surprised to see
driver.   him win the TT
                               Enduro Championship.

Below are three additional patterns with sample paragraphs after each:

#2 Generalization
        Particular Statement
        Particular Statement
        Particular Statement ⎫
Generalization   ⎬   Choice of One

Two sample paragraphs for the #2 pattern:

#2   Our old car sure is a bad one.
                    Yesterday the motor quit.
                    Today a wheel fell off.
[Choice ⎰ Tomorrow a door will probably break.
of One] ⎱ I guess it's just no good.

#2   Kenny Roberts is a superb motorcyclist.
                  He has won in flat track competition.
                      He often wins TT.
                  This year he even won the European
                Grand Prix of Motorcycling.
                      or
            Roberts is a consistent winner.

#3   Particular Statement
                  Particular Statement
                 Particular Statement
Generalization

Two sample paragraphs for the #3 pattern:

#3   Jimmy pulled my hair in class!
                  Yesterday he stole my apple.
                  At recess he threw rocks at me.
Boy, he sure is mean!

#3   Kenny Roberts just won the European
        Grand Prix of motorcycling.
            Earlier this year he won the Daytona Open.
    And last fall he won the U.S. Flat Track Open.

He is an excellent all-round Motorcycle Racer.

#4   Particular Statement
        Particular Statement
          Particular Statement
           Particular Statement
Generalization

Two sample paragraphs for the #4 pattern:

#4   I don't like peas!
              They're soft and mushy.
              They taste like gunk.
       They're just plain rotten!

#4   Kenny Roberts won the European Grand Prix of motorcycling.
              He had to work at the last minute to get his
                      cycle ready for the race.
              The suspension system was causing him problems.
              However, he got the suspension problem solved.
                                              or
       Roberts is a driver who performs well under pressure.

Possible Applications:

1. Find paragraphs in your textbooks that fit these patterns. Tell why you think they do.

2. Write original paragraphs using each of the four models.

Exchange paragraphs with a classmate and see whether you can tell which paragraphs fit which paragraph patterns.

Building narrative paragraphs by abstraction levels   Ask students to read the paragraph in Figure 6–1, which was written by a sixth-grader.

Now read the same paragraph in a form where sentences have been indented and numbered to show which ones are more general or more particular than others.

1. A place that is of importance to me is Camp Bear Paw.
2. Bear Paw is up near Mountain, Wisconsin.
3. At the camp you live in tents for a week.
4. There is an archery and rifle range for you to practice shooting at targets.

Figure 6–1.

> A place that is of importance to me is Camp Bear Paw. Camp Bear Paw is up near Mountain, Wisconsin. At the camp you live in tents for a week. There is an archery and rifle range for you to practice shooting at targets. There is also a lake to swim and go boating and fishing in. You get to eat in a mess hall. The camp is in a forest full of wildlife. There are trails to hike on through the forest. They have pieces of wood to walk on if you want to go through the log and look at the plants.

5. There is also a lake to swim and go boating and fishing in.
6. You get to eat in a mess hall.
7. The camp is in a forest full of wildlife.
8. There are trails to hike on through the forest.
9. They have pieces of wood to walk on if you want to go through the bog on one of the trails and look at plants.

Ask students whether they think this paragraph is well written. Why or why not? Notice that all, or nearly all, of the sentences are at the same general level. Sentences 2 through 8 are less general than the topic sentence, #1, but only sentence 9 is less general than sentences 2 through 8.

One way to write some sentences that are less general is to write sentences that contain details that help to describe or explain those sentences that come before them.

For example, what are some sentences that you could write about statement 7 that could be placed after 7 and before 8? Could you tell about particular wildlife that can be found at Camp Bear Paw?

If a paragraph has too many general sentences and not enough particular ones, what happens to the reader's interest?

Try to write a paragraph that starts with a general statement, followed by one less general, and then three or four more particular that are about your second general statement. Look at the following paragraph as an example:

1. One of my favorite places is Camp Possum Trot.
2. I especially like to eat at the mess hall there.
3. It is built like an old logger's dining hall.
4. The mess hall food is excellent tasting.
5. The cook is always friendly, too.

Discuss with students the difference in paragraphs ending with a generalization as opposed to those ending with a particular statement. (Perhaps paragraphs ending with generalizations more often conclude compositions or stand alone.)

Ask students to read a passage such as that in Figure 6–2.

If we were to outline the writing with sentences numbered and indented to show level of generality, it might look like this:

1st ¢
1. We go deer hunting at Black River Falls, and the land has always been special to me.
2. As you walk through the forest you can hear small birds jumping in the branches of the trees.
3. When it gets really cold, the old dead trees pop.
4. It sounds like they're trying to shoot at the hunters.
5. If you walk down the road we camp on, there is a small river.
6. It is a nice place to sit and watch for deer.

2nd ¢
7. Another place we go is on top of this big hill.
8. You can see a long way.
9. I think just being out in nature is just as fun as hunting.

Figure 6–2.

> We go deer hunting at Black River
> Falls, and the land has always been
> special to me. As you walk through the
> forest you can hear small birds jumping
> in the branches of the trees. When it
> gets really cold, the old dead trees pop.
> It sounds like they're trying to shoot
> back at the hunters.
>   If you walk down the road we camp
> on, there is a small river. It is a
> nice place to sit and watch for deer.
> Another place we go is on top of this
> big hill. You can see a long way.
>   I think just being out in nature is
> just as fun as the hunting.

Ask students questions designed to focus on the relationship of structure to content. For example, Do you think this is a good paper? Does the writer stick to the topic? Do you think the closing sentence could be improved? What are some of the things that make this effective writing?

One thing the author does is to create a word picture for us by using a pattern in which particular sentences provide detail about those that precede them. Why is the first paragraph more effective than the second one? How might you improve the second one?

Notice that activities such as these require the student to work with patterns of language structure and use that are characteristic of narration. Developing skills in using these patterns should be a part of the comprehensive writing program in the intermediate and middle school grades.

Ideas for Expository Writing in the Primary Grades

Reportive Reportive writing, you will recall, is basically objective description with minimum imposition of the writer's personal opinions.

Activities such as the following will help primary grade children develop the necessary skills in this mode of writing.

Provide students with handouts of a map you have made of a typical town. Include key locations such as the police and fire departments, hospitals, the post office, businesses such as banks, and other important places. Also make up fictitious residences and names of people. Have the students write a set of directions on how to get from one place to another with enough detail that a reader could actually follow the route on the map.

Provide a photograph of a scene full of activity, excitement, and detail. Ask the students to write two paragraphs, one a straightforward accurate description of the scene, the second a deliberately biased or subjective portrayal (for example, if people are involved, take a position that flatters one or, say, that attributes causes of an incident or event to a specific person).

This latter activity is useful for the student to begin to develop a sense of difference between exposition and narration in terms of the writer's personal feelings.

Ask students to write reports on trips, events, books read, TV shows or movies seen, or an important personal experience (for example, a parade or a trip to a zoo or park). As in the last activity, children can be asked to write two accounts, one objective or neutral in tone, the other flavored with their own point of view.

Have children work in pairs to prepare written reports on assigned research projects for which you have resource materials, for example, describing a breed of dog or cat or presenting a history of football or baseball. Depending upon the amount of time available, you may turn this into a major project, using notes, outlines, and other materials.

Have children maintain notes or records in a journal or manual recording their observations over time of a science experiment or perhaps plans for an activity. At the end of the project, ask them to write a description of the highlights of the experiment or activity.

Persuasive   Persuasive writing is more complex than reportive writing. It requires more careful and logical organization. Skill in persuasive writing develops gradually over the years in a well-articulated composition program. Activities such as these should help provide basic skills in this mode.

• Have the class divide into groups of four to five students. Present them with a problem to be resolved or a decision to be made, preferably a real one. It should be relatively easy to present a challenging realistic problem. For example, ask the children to suppose that their class had earned $50 through a cookie sale. They can use the money either to buy a gerbil as a class pet or to take a class trip to the zoo. Appoint a leader and recording secretary for each group. Have the groups brainstorm and list reasons for and against one proposal or another. Later these notes can be used to organize a written argument for the use of the money. Such a paper can be composed as a group project, or students can write individual papers, with each writer using duplicated copies of the notes generated in discussion.

• Present students with the following structural model for persuasive writing. The content can be adjusted according to the abilities of the child.

What sentence:
   1. We should buy a gerbil for our classroom.
Why sentences:
   2. Our class had a cookie sale, and we made $50.00.
   3. All the children agreed to take turns feeding and caring for the new pet.
So sentence:
   4. So, we will get our gerbil next week.

Initially, compose a paragraph such as the one above, with the class providing sentences while you write them on the board. Discuss the order of the *why* sentences and how some sentences suggested perhaps do not help the *what* sentence.

Then, using dittoed handouts, have children progress through the following exercises:

1. What are possible *so* sentences for the following?

What sentence: Our car is in bad shape.
Why sentences: The fenders are rusty.
                    The lights don't work.
                    The engine is noisy.

So sentence: Choose one and tell why it is best.
a. So, the doors creak.
b. So, we need a new car.
c. So, the paint is faded.

2. Below are some sentences that include a *what* sentence, *why* sentences, and a *so* sentence. They are mixed up. Write the sentences so that the *what* sentence is first, the *why* sentences follow, and the *so* sentence comes at the end.

a. You can swim then.
b. I like summer.
c. You can play ball then.
d. It is the best time of the year.

3. Below is a *what* sentence and some *why* sentences. We need a *so* sentence. See if you can write one.

What sentence: We had fun on the picnic.
Why sentences: There was fried chicken and homemade ice cream.
                    We played ball.
                    All of my friends were there.
So sentence:

4. Below is a *what* sentence and a *so* sentence. We need some *why* sentences between them. See how many good ones you can write.

What sentence: We have a good ball team.
Why sentences: 1.
                    2. . . .

So sentence (conclusion):   This is why I think we have the best team.

5. Below is a *what* sentence. Write some good *why* sentences and a *so* sentence.

What sentence: I like Christmas time best.
Why sentences: 1.
                   2. . . .
So sentence:

6. Use our *What-Why-So* sentence order to write about something you believe or like.

What sentence:
Why sentences: 1.
                   2. . . .
So sentence:

Note that the *What-Why-So* model is a very basic persuasive framework that can be modified for use at any grade. This gives it tremendous power and makes it one of the most important for students to master.

Persuasive Writing in the Intermediate/Middle School Grades

By the time children move into the intermediate and middle school grades, they should have developed the more fundamental persuasive writing skills. Further, their cognitive development is well enough advanced for them to reason hypothetically and conditionally, and utilize the more sophisticated sentence and paragraph structures and forms central to effective persuasive writing.

Although there are wide-ranging thinking and writing skills involved in persuasive writing, certainly ability to reason logically and organize compositions in a logically cohesive fashion must be accorded dominant importance. The following activities and ideas are intended to highlight these more critical skills.

• Build on the activities in the section on narrative writing, that is, distinguishing between particular assertions and generalizations, by discussing selected generalizations. For example, consider the following: (1) All redheads have tempers. (2) Wading barefooted in a ditch of cold water causes colds. (3) Crime never pays. (4) If you work hard, you will earn a lot of money. Discuss these statements with students by asking such questions as: (1) Are the statements true? How do you know? (2) How might you go about proving them true or false? (3) What happens when we use terms like *good, bad, best, worst, prettiest,* etc. in our language.

• Have students choose a TV commercial, describe its content and organization, and point out why it is or is not effective.

• Provide extensive practice for students identifying and writing cause-effect sentences. For example, in the sentences below, underline the "cause" part of the sentence with one line and the "effect" part with two lines.

1. We won't win because our pitcher is ill.
2. Because of the bad weather, the game was postponed.
3. The picnic is cancelled since the weather is bad.
4. If you study, you'll pass.
5. You can be successful if you try hard.
6. You hit me and I'll tell my Mommy!

Discuss with students how cause-and-effect order in sentences can be varied and how key words serve as cause-effect order cues, for example, *because, if-then, since*.

Have students produce sentences reflecting cause-effect relationships.

Ask students to paraphrase famous quotes or assertions that reflect cause-effect relationships. For example:

Ralph Waldo Emerson—"To be great is to be misunderstood."
(If one is great, he is misunderstood.)
Proverbs—"Of a good beginning cometh a good end."
(If you have a good beginning, you'll end up all right.)
Descartes—"I think, therefore I am."
(If you think, then you exist.)
G. B. Shaw—"A government that robs Peter to pay Paul can always depend on the support of Paul."
(If you always help one group, they'll probably support you.)

Have the students make up some possible "famous quotes," which reflect cause-effect relationships, then exchange quotes with a friend and rewrite the friend's quotes as "regular" cause-effect sentences.

• Provide students with deductive argument forms that have missing conclusions or premises. Ask them to write in appropriate ones.

1. The bread will rise only if yeast has been used. The bread is not rising. Therefore, _____.

2. Unless we live near the lake, summer will seem especially hot. We can't afford a lakeside home, so _____.

3. Either Jane or Peter will lead the choir. Jane has moved away. So, _____.

4. If car sales do not increase, the economy will suffer. _____, therefore the economy will suffer.

Refine and amplify the *What-Why-So* model offered for the primary grades in order to extend its use to older students. Specifically, convert the basic model into a "claim-support-conclusion" one. Below are samples revealing the best approaches.

1. The following paragraph has a claim sentence and support sentences. It does not have a conclusion sentence. See how many you can write.

Claim sentence: Many schools are not prepared to offer important physical activities for their students.

Support sentences: For example, few schools have indoor swimming pools, even though winter weather is too cold for children to swim outdoors. Many schools do

not include golf or fishing instruction in their physical education programs, although they are important sports in later life. Most children do not have a chance to participate in the most important sports in today's society. Therefore . . .
Conclusion sentence(s): 1.
  2. . . .

2. Below are a number of sentences that include a claim sentence, support sentences, and a conclusion sentence. They are mixed up. Write the sentences in a paragraph so that the claim sentence is first, the support sentences next, and the conclusion sentence at the end.

  a. There has been a lot of rain.
  b. The spring came earlier than usual this year.
  c. We did not have any late frost.
  d. Our corn crop will be a good one this year.
  e. It looks like we will do very well.
  f. The corn weevil has not been a problem this summer.

Write your paragraph below using the above sentences.

_____

_____

_____

_____

_____

3. Below are a claim sentence and a conclusion sentence. Support sentences need to be written that will logically connect them. Write several to produce a good paragraph.
Claim sentence: Our school will have a good basketball team this year.

  Support sentences: 1.
    2. . . .

Conclusion sentence: Because of these things, I think we have a good chance to be conference champs.

4. Choose a claim sentence from the following. Write several support sentences for it and end your writing with a conclusion sentence.

  1. Our school vacation should be longer.
  2. I like to shop for Christmas gifts for my family.
  3. I would like to live on a deserted island for a summer.
  4. Running everyday is good for you.

5. Use the claim-support-conclusion model to write a paper that will persuade a selected audience to believe you or act as you direct.
Claim sentence:

> Support sentences: 1.
>   2. . . .
> Conclusion sentence:

• After students have developed basic skills in employing the claim-support-conclusion model, variations of the model should be considered. Of most importance is developing the ability to organize and sequence the supporting sentences between the claim sentence and conclusion sentence. Support sentences reflect their own sequencing requirements in order for the paragraph or composition to be effective. For example, consider the following argument:
Claim sentence: Eighth-graders should be allowed to have a Halloween dress-up party at school.
Support sentences:

1. The eighth grade makes up the last year of our education before becoming high school students.
2. That is important, because as ninth-graders we will not be allowed to have that kind of party in our school.
3. The high school does not allow parties during the school day.
4. Also it is important to be with old friends for that kind of party.
5. And we'll be new students as ninth-graders in a new building.

Conclusion statement: So, I think the eighth grade is a good year to have a school dress-up party at Halloween.

Notice that sentence 2 in the support group could not logically be transposed with sentence 1, inasmuch as the word *that* refers to something previous. Notice, too, that sentence 4, introduced by the word *also,* and sentence 5, introduced by the word *and,* need supporting sentences before them for reference.

The logical fit of the "support sentences" group needs to be stressed in the middle school grades as a refinement. Overall, the teacher in these later elementary years needs to combine efforts in developing skills for writing logically sound sentences with those oriented toward writing logically sound paragraphs and compositions.

Ideas for Creative Writing
in the Primary Grades

Creative writing is the most direct personal written expression in which a writer reflects feelings, and that reflection of feeling transcends form. For the primary grade child especially, this mode of written expression is critical. Consider, in creative writing:

the child need not worry about audience, for the focus of the writing is self and expression of that self;

the child need not be intimidated by appearance of the writing, for appearance is secondary in the process at this stage of the child's writing skill development;

the child has the widest range of possible topics, purposes, and methods in producing writing in the creative mode.

Implicit in the above are certain ideas the teacher should keep in mind. Of particular concern are postures the classroom teacher should take in this mode of written expression that may not be applicable in others. For example, in general:

the child should have wide latitude in choosing subjects about which to write and, to whatever extent possible, the form the writing should take and the time and place for its production;

the child's creative writing ought *not* to be evaluated or critiqued on its presentational amenities (mechanics);

the child should *not* be required to share creative writing results (most children in this age range do enjoy sharing their writing; however, that option not to should always be theirs); and

in creative writing as a *teaching device,* the self-discovery, or self-learning, is *always* central, the quality of the written product secondary.

Following are ideas for teaching creative writing in each of the creative modes—prose, poetry, and drama:

STORY STARTERS

Provide children with:

openings to stories (and ask them to complete the story)
"Once upon a time there was an old house in the forest. A ghost named Herman lived there . . ."
character descriptions
"Zeke was a tired old man who lived alone in a cabin high in the mountains. One day he was out walking when a strange thing happened . . ."

or

"Mary Ann was surprised when she opened the door . . ."
critical points
"Then suddenly the door opened . . ."

or

"Bill jumped for the boat just as it pulled away from the dock . . ."

Poetry forms   Haiku poetry is a seventeenth-century Japanese poetry form that children in the second and third grades can master. Haiku consists of 17 syllables on 3 lines, in a 5-7-5 syllable combination, and focuses upon a single theme—usually nature. For example:

The pink swamp flower
Has a beauty of its own—
A heavy fragrance.

or

The tiny brown mouse
Cold, nervous and tired—
A sad, sorry, sight.

or

The big yellow sun
Was bright and very warm—
Staring on the earth.

Provide several samples for the children. Do not dwell on exact syllable count. Get the children to play with the rhythm and general word count per line. Also the idea of sticking to one theme is important.

Cinquain poetry, though not Japanese in origin, is similar in some respects to the haiku form. It, too, addresses a central theme—often in nature—and does not rhyme. The cinquain has 5 lines with 22 syllables distributed in the pattern 2-4-6-8-2. For example:

The gull
effortlessly
glides on the downward breeze
to land on the soft, sandy beach:
Quiet.

A simpler version is to base the form upon word count rather than syllable count, for example:

1st line = 1 word
2nd line = 2 words
3rd line = 3 words
4th line = 4 words
5th line = 1 word

For example:

Mouse
Tiny fur
Quiet, soft animal
Running in the grass
Cute

An important point to remember is that exact form compliance is not essential and should not be emphasized in the primary grades. The haiku, cinquain, and all other poetry forms should be seen as directional guides, in principle, rather than as prescriptions to be mastered in technical detail.

Ideas for Creative Writing in the Intermediate and Middle School Grades

To some extent the major difference between writing instruction in the creative mode between primary and later grades is in the degree of sophistication and the approach rather than the content per se. For example, haiku and cinquain poetry are elegant poetry forms and excellent instructional models throughout the years. They should be kept as part of the creative writing mode in the later grades.

However, there are also other more demanding creative writing skills and concepts reserved largely for later grades. Following are a variety of ideas for developing these abilities, ranging from individual creative vocabulary development to instruction in longer creative expressive modes.

• Writing "concrete poems" can be fun—see Figure 6–3! Write a concrete poem by first thinking of a picture of some action, then make up a poem to fit the picture (a challenging activity!).

Some Word Play Ideas

Hinky-Pinkies—a two-syllables-per-word rhyming two-word phrase that redefines (easy to explain to students simply by example).

A tired flower   = A lazy daisy or a dozy posey
A fish doctor   = A sturgeon surgeon
A book that has eyes = A look book

For greater challenge, what are some

"Hinkety-Pinketies"?

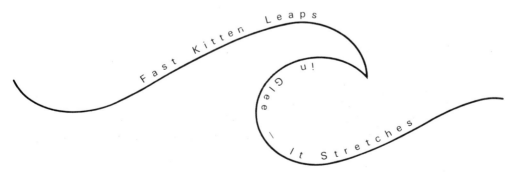

Figure 6–3.

or

"Rinky-Dinky-Hinky-Pinkies"?

Jonathan Swifties, for example:

"He sure is honest, said Lincoln, *ably*."
or
"The knife is dangerous, he said *sharply*."
or
"My car has a flat, he said *tiredly*."

Animate-Inanimate Word Charts—Word charts that posit analogies between animate and inanimate objects may be useful learning devices. For example:

ACTIONS OF A CAR

CAR	PERSON
starts	gets up in the morning
stalls	is tired
washed and polished	dressed up

These can be made up by students, kept on file cards in shoeboxes, with cards arranged alphabetically or according to theme, and can be used as idea starters for poems or stories.

Mixing Metaphors

For example:

As fast as an orange sleeps,
As pretty as _____?

Adjective Charting

WORDS	SWEET	WARM	ORANGE	TALL	COLD	PRETTY
dog						
flower						
radio						
car						

Students fill out each cell in the matrix with the word phrase resulting from the noun column with the adjective columns. Each row then has interesting and often unusual phrases, for example, *sweet dog*.

Have students create their own adjective charts. Again, these can be stored on file cards and used in the writing center.

Word Sounds. For example:

Z iiiii nnnn ggg
the word sped by

W W o o o o F F F
said the big dog

yiip
said the little puppy

Writing Plays and Scripts
Through the Elementary Grades

Writing plays or scripts for plays is an excellent means to develop a wide range of composing skills as well as cooperation skills. However, this area of creative writing is also one of the most demanding; hence, individual practice in the other writing areas through activities suggested elsewhere should precede the writing of scripts and plays.

Points of departure: creative drama   Use creative drama activities as springboards into play script writing. Have the students work in pairs or small teams to transcribe their improvisations into written form.

Creative drama activities should move from minimal-demand-on-participant types to more complex. For example, brief one-person pantomimes can develop out of show-and-tell. These pantomimes can then be done in pairs, with the two students collaborating on what each will do.

Larger and more complex creative dramas should be largely interpretive in nature initially. For example, the teacher can set up the plot line, the characters' personalities, and other aspects of the setting. The students then simply interpret creatively what is given. As they get more experience in interpretive creative dramatics, they can begin more improvisational efforts where they establish increasingly the context and direction of their production.

Points of departure: stories and scripts   Provide the students with story outlines, that is, the basic plot and character profiles. Have the students write dialogue for the characters so that the story can be acted out as a play. With older students, remind them of need for direction, for the strategic placement on stage of props and characters at certain points. Alternatively, provide students with an incomplete play script you have written and ask them to complete it. Have the students compare their different versions in small groups. A final variant is to use field trips, talks by visitors, or school events and activities for class brainstorming to produce ideas for plays.

Script producing   Provide cartoons, photographs, or comic strips for the students—but with no dialogue. Have them write appropriate dialogue or narrative for each picture in the sequence.

After students have done this a few times, have them write the dialogue on regular writing tablets without the comic-strip pictures. Talk about whether there is enough information in their scripts. What information was provided visually by the graphics that is not in their written dialogue? What needs to be added to the scripts in writing to make up for the absent pictures? Such questions help students begin thinking about the fact that play scripts must contain more than just dialogue alone—namely, character description and exposition of where and when to use props. Another related activity would be to divide the students into work teams and have them talk about how writing tasks for a play might be assigned.

Sequencing play writing according to play type difficulty   Written plays need not be long or complex. Initial play script writing can focus upon two-character dialogue in a brief scene. The teacher can even make this exercise easier by providing dittoed handouts that detail the setting and dialogue at least partially. For example:

> Scene: A mother and her little girl are sitting in the living room early one evening after dinner. The mother has just read a funny story to her child.
> MOTHER: Well, how did you like the story?
> LITTLE GIRL:
> MOTHER:
> LITTLE GIRL: . . .

This activity can be easily shortened or extended by adjusting the number of character leads provided.

Play writing can then move to the addition of more and more characters even in the context of one scene or one act. Multiple-scene scripts should come only after much practice and considerable experience. Usually this can start in the intermediate grades if there has been some basic script writing experience in the primary grades. In sequencing script types, one should note that radio productions are easier to script than TV, movie, or live performances, since only sound effects and voice control are essential with the former. Remember, too, that TV or radio or live role-playing scripts can be very imitative and deal with things such as quiz shows and news programs.

The teacher in the elementary grades must remember that skill in this mode of written expression is far-reaching and a powerful base for all *writing types, and the basics of creative writing should be developed in the elementary grades if later efforts are to be fruitful.*

SELECTED REFERENCES
FOR TEACHING VARIOUS
DISCOURSE MODES

KOCH, K.   *Wishes, Lies, and Dreams.* New York: Vintage Books, 1970.
KOCH, K.   *Rose, Where Did You Get That Red?* New York: Vintage Books, 1973.
KLEIN, M.   *Talk in the Language Arts Classroom.* Urbana: NCTE/ERIC, 1977.
MOFFETT, J. and WAGNER, B. J.   *Student-Centered Language Arts and Reading, K–13.* Boston: Houghton Mifflin, 1983.
STEWIG, J.   *Read to Write.* New York: Hawthorn Books, 1975.

ELEMENTS OF WRITING

The heart of the writing process is the writer's ability to use the various discourse modes for a variety of purposes and audiences. Style and adaptability are thus musts for the effective writer. However, if those abilities are composition's heart, then its base or roots are the ability to produce sentences that are clear, straightforward, and concise at a minimum, and varied, elegant, and selectively chosen at best. The elements of writing—syntax, language uses, and the logic of language—are where careful and adequate instruction and practice can assure handsome dividends of written competency for the young writer.

Syntax (Sentence Structure)

Activities intended to help the elementary school student develop facility in employing syntax grammatical structures must comprehend all five major sub-categories of our composition curriculum framework—namely, parts of speech, coordination, predication, modification, and subordination.

The following activities all utilize formats amenable to teaching the relevant sentence writing skills. What they have in common is that nearly all place the student in a learning context where the main emphasis is on sentence *production* rather than sentence *analysis*. A second feature of these formats is that there is no necessary commitment to the teaching of any formal grammar terminology. However, the teacher can note various places where it would be an easy matter to teach formal terminology if there is a desire or need to do so.

SLOTTING, FRAMING, EMBEDDING, AND EXPANDING SENTENCES, SENTENCE PARTS, AND SENTENCE PATTERNS

For parts of speech   The terms in the above heading are often used interchangeably or for slightly different purposes to describe techniques for teaching elements of sentence structure. They are all quite similar, however, in that they ask the student to "close" or "fill in" or "flesh out" a sentence with blanks or spaces provided. For example:

"The little ducks _____."
waddled
scooted
walked
trotted
ran

(The student chooses the most appropriate verb to complete the sentence.) Variations on this activity:

1. Use the format above—with some slots for verbs, some for adjectives, and some for nouns—on dittoed handouts and ask the children to complete them individually, in pairs, or through group decision-making orally in groups of three to five.

2. Write the frame sentence on the board. Then brainstorm with the children and list their options for the frame. Discuss with them how the meaning or effect of the sentence is altered by different choices.

3. Have students write their own frame sentences with alternative slot or frame fillers, then exchange papers and fill in the frames on the other child's paper.

Other examples to consider:

"The _____ man ran fast."
old
strange
little   alternative adjective choices
nice

Or,

"The dog ate the bone _____."

adverb choices   {quickly
                        {rapidly
                        {slowly

prepositional phrase choices   {in a hurry
                                {with gusto

adverbial clause choices   {while staring at the boy
                           {when the girl left

Or,

_____ is funny.

The little kitten
The old barn   } noun phrase choices
A green frog

The boy's kite flying
The kitten's belly-scratching } *gerund nominals
The man's eating

*Nominals are words or groups of words used to function as nouns, for example, serving as subjects or direct objects in a sentence. Gerunds are verb forms ending in -ing and used as nouns. Infinitives are the word to plus the verb used as a noun.

To run backwards
To eat persimmons } *infinitive nominals
To lick ice cubes

FRAMING/SLOTTING FOR GRAMMATICAL FUNCTION

Conjoining/Coordinating/Paralleling

1. _____ and _____ went to town.
2. Mary said that she wanted to _____ and to _____.
3. The car hit the _____ but missed the _____.

The above samples provide practice with nouns or noun phrases as compound subjects (1), infinitives as objects (2), and nouns or noun phrases as objects (3).

More challenging types can require the learner to use contrasting parallelism (as in 4, below) or parallel clauses (as in 5, below). Note that such activities designed to assist in the teaching of extended parallelism as well as those for teaching subordination and use of relative clauses are most appropriately reserved for the upper elementary and middle school grades.

4. Mary _____ and Joe _____ when their friend moved away.
5. The President said, " _____," and _____, but _____.

Subordinating

1. After _____, you may play.
2. The children were unhappy because _____.
3. I like to run if _____.

The subordinating usages above are quite demanding cognitively. Therefore, students should have considerable practice with simpler grammatical constructs prior to having to deal with subordination.

Modifying (producing sentences using who, which, that)

1. I know that _____.
2. I want the one which _____.
3. Jane is the girl who _____.
4. "Who _____?" asked the little man.
5. I like the teacher who _____.

Additional more challenging relative clause sentences are:

6. I like the car that _____ because it _____.
7. The old man who _____ knew that _____.

Inductive experiments for inferring and applying grammatical structures   A useful activity for helping children discover certain linguistic attributes of their own grammar system is to utilize an inductive experiment format where example serves to provide both definition and direction. For example:

Experiment:	*The Order of Words in Sentences*
Given:	1. "The cat ate a rat" is a sentence.
	2. "A ate rat cat the" is *not* a sentence.
	3. "The car leaks oil" is a sentence.
	4. "Leaks car oil the" is *not* a sentence.
Material:	Now look at this:
	1. mile a Dan ran
	2. Dan ran mile a
	3. tree the fell
	4. Bill took a pill
Directions:	Read the groups of words in "*Material*." Now answer the following questions:
	1. Which are sentences?
	2. Which ones are not sentences?

_____
_____
_____
_____

Conclusion:	For a group of words to be a sentence, words must be in the correct _____.
Application:	Rewrite the groups of words in "*Material*" that are *not* sentences so that they become sentences.

Or, for teaching adjective attributes and roles in sentences:

Experiment:	*Simple Describing Words in Sentences*
Given:	1. A funny boy ate his orange.
	"Funny" is a describing word.
	2. Joan wore a pretty coat.
	"Pretty" is a describing word.
Material:	1. The young nurse ran 5 miles.
	2. The old wagon had square wheels.
	3. A saggy bag was filled with junk.
	4. The boy left town.
Direction:	Read the sentences in "*Material*."
	1. Do they all have describing words (words like *funny* or *pretty*)? _____.
	2. Underline the describing words in the sentences.

Conclusion: 1. Can you have sentences without describing words?
_____ .

Application: 1. Write two sentences with describing words.

_____

_____

An experiment demonstrating sentence-building with clause-length grammatical constructs for use with older students is the following:

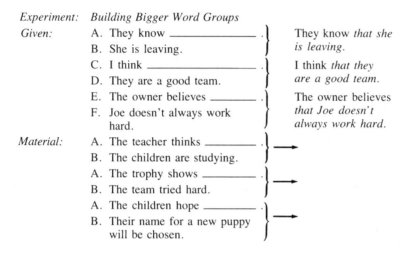

Experiment: *Building Bigger Word Groups*

Given: A. They know _____ .   They know *that she*
           B. She is leaving.   *is leaving.*
           C. I think _____ .   I think *that they*
           D. They are a good team.   *are a good team.*
           E. The owner believes _____ .   The owner believes
           F. Joe doesn't always work   *that Joe doesn't*
              hard.   *always work hard.*

Material: A. The teacher thinks _____ .   →
            B. The children are studying.
            A. The trophy shows _____ .   →
            B. The team tried hard.
            A. The children hope _____ .   →
            B. Their name for a new puppy
               will be chosen.

The "Experiment" format can be used to teach comprehension and limited application of grammatical constructs with a wide range of syntactic complexity and sophistication throughout the grades.

Its particular advantages are several:

1. Students have the opportunity to "discover" important linguisic attributes of their language system, a system they unconsciously employ but do not yet consciously know.
2. It is less didactic than the lessons typically found in basal texts and workbooks.
3. The discovery process is one of personal involvement. The process of discovering the features and attributes of our language system is more fundamental than being able to demonstrate that we know the formal attributes of the language system exhibited.
4. The concept of discovery is essentially in keeping with the concept of teaching the nature of language as a living, changing system whose features are not fixed in stone.

Sentence-combining   Of the various techniques for teaching sentence structure, that which is most often cited as one rooted in research is sentence-combining. Sentence-combining is the practice of taking a series of short choppy sentences and combining them into one by deleting some words and, sometimes, changing others.

The simplest variety of sentence-combining clusters is the "open-ended" type. For example:

1. The dress was pretty.
   The dress was blue.
   The dress was new.
   The dress was in the closet.

   The pretty new dress was in the closet.

2. The puppy was cute.
   The puppy was mean.
   The puppy ate the food.
   The food was soggy.

   The cute mean puppy ate the soggy food.

3. The girl drank the soda.
   The girl was little.
   The girl was in the booth.
   The soda was sweet.

   The little girl in the booth drank the sweet soda.

4. The rain fell on the street.
   The rain was slow.
   The rain was chilly.
   The street was narrow.
   The street was old.

   The slow chilly rain fell on the old narrow street.

A more structured version is the "cued" variety where a cue word is placed in parentheses after the sentence that is to be altered using the cue word. The word can be added, as with the relative pronoun in the following cluster:

1. The kids were tired.
2. The kids were hungry. (who)
Result: "The kids who were hungry were tired."

Or the cue word can be a verb changed to produce a participial modifer, for example:

1. The girl was happy.
2. The girl sipped a soda. (sipping)
Result: "The girl sipping a soda was happy."

Sentence-combining clusters can be designed in simple or easy sets or can be made more challenging by increasing the number of sentences to be combined, by scrambling the order of those to be combined, or by varying the difficulty or complexity of cue words provided.

Further, sentence-combining can be utilized to teach particular grammatical constructs implicitly (by choice of sentences to be combined in the open-ended types), for example:

1. The team lost the game.
2. Their pitcher was ill.

These sentences provide the student with combining choices geared toward use of a causal clause, that is:

The team lost the game because their pitcher was ill.

Research indicates that use of sentence-combining in conjunction with other elements of a writing program will significantly improve sentence writing skills.

SOME IDEAS FOR SENTENCE-COMBINING ACTIVITIES IN THE PRIMARY GRADES

1.   Cluster sentence-combining sets according to themes, for example, Halloween and other holidays.

   a. The witch rode a broom.
   b. The witch was ugly.
   c. The broom was floppy.
         or
   a. Santa was jolly.
   b. Santa was chubby.
   c. Santa brought gifts.

2. Provide sentence-combining sets focusing on different grammatical categories, for example, adjectives and adverbs.

   a. The dog was old.
   b. The dog was on the road.
         or
   a. The children ran.
   b. The children ran across the yard.
   c. The children ran fast.
         or
   a. A flower grew.
   b. It grew in the sunlight.
   c. The sunlight was bright.

(Notice that the last set is more challenging, encouraging children to use a relative pronoun, that is, "A flower grew in the sunlight *that* was bright"—although another possibility is "A flower grew in the bright sunlight," which is, in fact, a more economical sentence.)

3. Organize sentence-combining sets to produce a short story or paragraph when the sentences are ordered. For example:

   a. The coat was old.
      The coat was fur.
      It was in the closet.
   b. The boy put it on.
      The boy was in a hurry.
      The boy left.
   c. The boy went out to play.
      He played ball.
      He played with the children.

Possible result: The old fur coat was in the closet. The boy, who was in a hurry, put it on and left. He went out to play ball with the children.

4. Provide sentence-combining experiences with the "closed" variety.

   a. The girl likes *something.*
   b. The apples are green.

Possible result: The girl likes green apples.

SENTENCE-COMBINING IN THE LATER GRADES

1. Extend the list of clustered sentences to be combined and scramble their order to increase complexity.

   a. The lot was across the street.
   b. They were told not to.
   c. The lot was vacant.
   d. The boys went into the lot.

Possible result: Although they were told not to, the boys went into the vacant lot across the street. (*Or:* The boys, who were told not to, went into the vacant lot across the street.)

2. Incorporate "closed" and "cued" varieties.

   a. The tennis player raised her racket.
   b. She stared intently at her opponent. (staring)
   c. Her opponent was anxious.
   d. Her racket was new.

Possible result: Staring intently at her anxious opponent, the tennis player raised her new racket.

    a. *Something* was a surprise.
    b. Joe left the game. (for/to)
    c. The surprise was big.

Possible result: For Joe to leave the game was a big surprise.
3. Design activities emphasizing the use of subordination and relative pronouns.

    a. The doctor couldn't get to the hospital.
    b. He was in a traffic jam.
    c. The traffic jam was bad.
    d. The doctor was eager.

This cluster implicitly encourages use of subordination to reflect cause-effect. Possible result: The eager doctor couldn't get to the hospital because he was in a bad traffic jam.
Relative pronouns (who, which, that) can be built in by using them as cue words.

    a. The motorcycle raced down the track.
    b. The motorcycle belonged to Jerry. (that)
    c. The track was dirt.

Possible result: The motorcycle that belonged to Jerry raced down the dirt track.
4. Select a passage from a story or narrative the students are to read. Choose an opening sentence and break it into constituent basic sentences. Ask students to combine them. For example, consider these:

   1. A man walked up and down.
    2. The man was little.
    3. The man was fat.
    4. The man was old.
    5. The man walked nervously.
   6. The man was upon the veranda of a house.
    7. The veranda was half decayed.
    8. The house was small.
    9. The house was frame.
 10. The house stood near the edge of a ravine.
    11. The ravine was near the town of Winesburg, Ohio.

This produces an exceptionally long sentence, but one a well-known author felt appropriate. Discuss various student versions. How are they alike? How are they different? Are some more pleasing than others? Now, if one were writing a short story with a sad or tragic tone and the author wanted to establish such a mood for the story in this sentence, how would he write it? Which student's sentence sounds as if it would fit best in such a story?

Here is the original by Sherwood Anderson: "Upon the half decayed veranda of a small frame house that stood near the edge of a ravine near the town of Winesburg, Ohio, a fat little old man walked nervously up and down" (from "Hands," in *Winesburg, Ohio*). "Why does Anderson choose to construct the sentence this way? Why is his version effective?" are kinds of questions the teacher can use before pointing out that "Hands" is a tragic story about a pitiful man who has not coped well with self or others.

This particular activity is an excellent advance organizer for the reading of a story or assignment. Important characteristics of the author's thesis or main ideas can often be addressed with this sentence-combining technique. Some final suggestions on sentence-combining use:

1. If overused, sentence-combining can become tedious and drill-like. Use it frequently but only for short periods of time.
2. Vary instructional techniques with sentence-combining. Use the overhead projector for variety and to encourage whole class discussion. Also include small-group and paired activities.
3. Use it as *part* of the grammar and composition program, *not* as the whole program.

Uses of Language

One important aspect of language use that figures into the writing process but often goes unattended is that language serves different semantic or meaning roles. For example, there are differences between asserting or proclaiming with the language and asking or inquiring with it. And even within the asserting category there are varying types and forms the language can take. There are subtle differences between describing and explaining. For example, there are differences in the structure and role of particular assertions and generalizations. And, although many of the abilities for employing these various language expression types and forms are quite sophisticated, there are still a number of activities and techniques that can be introduced in the elementary grades to assist students in developing abilities to see the differences in the various assertion and non-assertion types and their uses. The following activities can assist in developing these abilities.

Ask students to identify which of the following sentences perform which functions (D = Describe; E = Explain; P = Propose).
1. The ball is red.
2. I want the ball to be red.
3. The ball is red because the paint used was red.

Write sentences describing an object or an event.

Write sentences that explain how to build something, how to do something, or how to get somewhere.

Write sentences which try to convince someone about something.

The above activities can be assisted by providing sentence-completion exercises such as the following:

> "I like _____."
> "I think that _____."
> "The dog looks like _____."
> "The little man _____."
> "We should save our money because _____."

Find samples of writing in newspapers, magazines, and books that are essentially reportive or descriptive in type, others that attempt to explain a process or activity, and others that attempt to persuade or propose an argument. Discuss the relationships among these kinds of sentences and the types of writing in which they appear.

Have students write paragraphs that incorporate the sentence types on related topics. For example, ask them first to write a paragraph describing their classroom as accurately as possible so a stranger might recognize it from the written description. As a follow-up, ask them to write a paragraph pointing out the most important feature or place in the room and explain why that is so. Finally, ask them to write a composition designed to propose a change in the room (a new paint job, additional plants) and try to persuade others. Later, ask the students to identify each type of sentence (describing, explaining, or proposing) in their papers and tell whether there are more of one type or another in each writing done. Talk about the differences in class.

The Logic of Language

In order to be an effective and efficient writer, the child must learn not only how to write quality sentences but also how to put them together so that they cohere or stand as a whole, each contributing to the power and usefulness of those preceding and following. Recent national assessment of writing of children (ages 9, 13, and 17) reveals that this is one of the more serious weaknesses in their writing—an inability to effectively sequence sentences one after the other so there is logical development, unity, and coherence in the written piece. *In short, writing mastery includes the ability to capitalize effectively upon both intrasentence relationships and intersentence relationships.*

Some ideas for teaching sequencing

1. Write a brief paragraph (or more, for greater complexity) in the following style:

(1) The boy walked down the street. (2) Then he saw a car coming. (3) He decided to wait until the car passed before he crossed the intersection.

Write the sentences in a numbered list but in scrambled order. Have the students rearrange them into the proper order.

Variations on this activity include:

writing the sentences on cardboard strips—then rearranging can be done by simply reordering the strips;

clipping cartoon sequences or drawing your own picture stories and having children order the pictures in proper sequence;

using stories or paragraphs written by students and scrambling them.

2. Use sentence combining in mixed array so that children have three tasks. First, they must reorder the array in proper sequence. Then they must decide how to cluster the sentences into related groups. And, finally, they should combine the sentences to produce a correctly sequenced paragraph. For example,

Given:

1. He raced along the road.
2. The road was narrow.
3. The boy jumped on the motorcycle.
4. The boy was big.
5. The garage was old.
6. The road was curvy.
7. The motorcycle was red.
8. He stopped by the garage.
9. The garage was near his home.

Reordered and sequenced, the array would look like the following:

1. The boy jumped on the motorcycle. ⎫
2. The boy was big.   ⎬ 1st cluster
3. The motorcycle was red.   ⎭
4. He raced along the road.   ⎫
5. The road was curvy.   ⎬ 2nd cluster
6. The road was narrow.   ⎭
7. He stopped by the garage.   ⎫
8. The garage was old.   ⎬ 3rd cluster
9. The garage was near his home.   ⎭

A three-sentence paragraph may then be constructed:

The big boy jumped on his red motorcycle. He raced along the narrow, curvy road. He stopped by the old garage near his home.

Notice that this activity can be made easier or more challenging by simply reducing or increasing the number or difficulty of sentences to be sequenced and combined. Also the amount of scrambling of array order can be reduced or increased.

SOME IDEAS FOR TEACHING UNITY AND COHERENCE

Using deductive logic Teach students the structure of two or three simple deductive argument forms. For argument, the disjunctive syllogism asserts:

1. Either A or B happens.
2. A does *not* happen.
3. Therefore, B happens.

1. "We are going either to the grocery store or to the post office."
2. "We are not going to have time to go to the grocery store."
3. "So we'll go to the post office instead."

Notice that we change the language a little when we write the disjunctive syllogism as a standard English language paragraph. However, the three main parts of the deductive argument are there.
• Provide students with disjunctive syllogisms with the assertions scrambled, for example:

1. We'll stay home.
2. We will not go to town.
3. Either we go to town or we stay home.

1. I did not have a cheese sandwich.
2. I had a ham sandwich.
3. Mother was going to make either a cheese sandwich or a ham sandwich for my lunch.

Have them reorder the assertions in the proper form.
• Provide disjunctive syllogisms with one or two missing assertions and ask children to make up appropriate ones:

1. John goes to either the red school or the white school.
2. He said he did not go to the red school.
3. So, I guess he goes ―――――――――.

Or,

1. Either we go on a picnic or we'll go to the zoo.
2. ―――――――――.
3. So, ―――――――――.

Another argument form that elementary school students learn easily is the Modus Ponens. It appears like this:

1. If A happens, then B will happen.

2. A happens.
3. So, B also happens.

In more straightforward language,

> If the weather is nice, we'll go on a picnic. The sun is shining and it's warm out. So, I think we'll go for the picnic.

The same kinds of activities suggested for the disjunctive syllogism may be used with the Modus Ponens.

Using cohesive ties   Sentences cohere or are "tied together" in writing in a number of ways. Back-and-forward referencing is one means. This is often accomplished through the use of particular transition words such as *they, so, after, before, and, but,* and *since.* Such terms also help paragraphs to cohere.

One of the most common and important cohesion devices, however, is the pronoun. Notice the use of pronouns in the following:

> The lion jumped out of (its) cage. (It) then ran across the street where several people were standing. (They) quickly ran away because (they) feared (him.)

Pronouns enable the reader and writer to refer back to previously established ideas without being unduly repetitious. They also enable the reader and writer to think ahead to approaching referents or ideas. For example:

> "*It* crashed through the window, then the (ball) rolled across the floor."

Students need to learn both to comprehend texts or passages utilizing pronominal and cue word cohesion and to produce cohesive writing with these devices serving as assists.

Following are some activities that can help in respect to both of these area.

Back-Referencing Sentences

Have students write a sentence for each of the following sentences using a pronoun (a word other than the one underlined). For example:

> "The *bird* ate the seeds."
>
> '(It) seemed happy."

1. The *kitten* chased the yarn.
2. _____ was cute.
1. The kitten chased the ball of yarn.
2. _____ unrolled on the floor.

Complete Paragraphs

Provide students with paragraphs that need to be completed by inserting the appropriate pronouns in the blanks.
For example:

Once upon a time a little old man lived alone in the
forest. _____ was kind and gentle, and the
animals all loved him. _____ would often come to
visit at _____ cottage. _____ would feed
_____ nuts and fruits.

Have the students fill in pronouns and then exchange papers to compare results.

Linking Sentences

Provide students with passages where an important transition sentence is missing. Ask them to make up one that is suitable for the slot provided. For example:

(1) The girl slid down the hill on her sled.
(2) She was having fun in the snow.
(3) All of a sudden a big tree was in front of her.
(4) _____.
(5) She laughed as the sled stopped.

Linking Paragraphs

Provide students with paragraphs that need intervening paragraphs to help them cohere into one complete text. Consider the following example:

p. 1 { The children enjoyed the trip to the zoo. They got to see many unusual animals they had never seen before.

p. 2 {

p. 3 { They decided that the anteater was the strangest even though they all liked the giraffes too.

In all of these activities it is important to consider the value of group and class discussion. Talking about what choices were made, why they were made, and how students knew what pronouns referred to what referents can help the learner grasp the concepts and skills central to writing cohesively.

SELECTED REFERENCES ON
THE USES AND LOGIC OF
LANGUAGE

HAYAKAWA, S. I. *Language in Thought and Action.* New York: Harcourt Brace Jovanovich, 1964.

HENNINGS, D. G. *Communication in Action: Teaching the Language Arts.* Boston: Houghton Mifflin, 1982.

MOFFETT, J., and WAGNER, B. *Student-Centered Language Arts and Reading.* Boston: Houghton Mifflin, 1983.

THE IMPINGING FACTORS OF
CIRCUMSTANCE

These are the factors over which the writer often has little control. Yet, they are important in the outcome of the final written product and must be considered during the writing.

Audience

Self-As-Audience

Take students on a hike through a meadow, park, or forest. Have each take a notebook and jot down notes about things observed. Tell them they will later use the notes to write about what they saw.

Ask students to pretend that they are going on a camping trip for the weekend and each is responsible for his or her own food and clothing. Have them prepare a list of things they will need for the trip.

Have students keep a daily journal that they need not share with anyone. They can keep the journal in their desk or locker and record things of importance to them only.

Ask students to close their eyes and listen to a sound you will make with selected objects from a group you have put together on your desk. Have the children open their eyes and jot down notes to help them remember later.

Personal-You-As-Audience

Have the students write a letter to a good friend. Ask them to use the notes they took on their trip to the park or forest and tell their friend about their experience.

Have the children write letters to a policeman friend or fireman or doctor, asking them to come to school and talk about their job.

Have the students talk about the difference in writing they do just for themselves and that which they might send to a friend.

Tell students they will be going out in the community to talk with some elderly people. Have students prepare questions that can be used to interview some older person to find out what the community was like many years ago.*

---

*If the reader is not familiar with the Foxfire projects directed by Eliot Wigginton, note the books by him in the recommended references following this section.

Unknown-You-As-Audience

Have the students write a description of their trip to the park or forest. Tell them that the piece will be used for the bulletin boards for parents' night so that they can find out about the trip.

Provide the students with large (5 × 8) lined note cards. Ask them to write descriptions of books they have read on these. Keep the cards filed (for example, in a shoe box) according to theme or type—mystery, humor, poetry—for other children to read if they would like to get some ideas about a book to choose for personal reading.

Ask students to use the responses they received in their oral interviews of the older people and write an account of what they learned. These will then be collected and organized into a class book. To make this a more extensive project, appoint students as editors and printers to produce a quality book or booklet.

Have children write original stories, poems, or plays that can be bound into a book to be shared with other classes, parents, or visitors.

Psychological Distancing

Place children into more extended writing projects that build from each other. For example, have them pretend that they went on a camping trip. A bear came into camp at night and caused a stir and commotion. "Jot down some notes to yourself that will help you remember the details of the event" (the first assignment). Then use those notes to write a letter to a personal friend who was ill and unable to go on the camping trip. Finally, the editor of the local paper has heard about the incident and would like to run a short article about it for the readers of the paper. Write a short article for the editor.

A similar activity with even greater student involvement is to have the class act as field anthropologists or sociologists. Have them use a cassette tape recorder to record an interview with a grandparent or someone in the family or community who knows something of historical interest about the local area. Have the students make notes from their tapes and then write up an account in narrative form. (They can jot down notes in a field journal instead of using a tape recorder if desired.) Collect these narratives and assemble them into a class journal.

Activities such as these help writers to develop a sense of audience and a feeling for some of the variations in writing style and structure that we employ to accommodate changes in our audience.

Setting and Subject

Our use of "setting" here should not be confused with the literary concept of setting. In composition instruction, setting refers to the degree of formality or informality required by the audience, subject, purpose, and context of the presentation. A composition written to be read by parents on the bulletin board or in a class book is far more formal than the notes entered by the student in his personal journal. The range of subjects may also vary considerably, from highly abstract to very concrete or specific ones.

In both setting and subject concept treatment, the teacher needs to remember the developmental level of the child. Primary grade children prefer to deal with concrete or specific subject matter but in a relatively informal mode. From the fourth grade on, students can be expected to address a wider range of subjects and cast them into appropriate settings.

The following activities should help students to develop skills in using these rhetorical notions by means of placing events in a time space.

List several things you did yesterday.

List some things you want to do tomorrow.

Tell the class some of the things you and a friend did last week.

Write several sentences beginning "Yesterday I _____."

Write several sentences beginning "Tomorrow I want to _____."

Write a short story about something that happened a long time ago.

Write a short story about a trip to a faraway planet that will happen many years from now.

Using ceremonial and formal language settings   The ability to relate language type and form to the setting, audience, and purpose intended is one that takes time and practice to master. However, foundations for this ability should be built in the elementary grades. Following are activities that should assist in this development.

Have students pretend they own a pet shop and want the people who work for them to be courteous to customers. Have them write down some things they would want their workers to say to every customer (for example, "Thank you for shopping at J Mart").

Have students pretend to be police officers giving a talk to fourth-graders on bike safety while traveling to school. Be sure to have them use a stern and serious look!

Have students role-play a scene involving a judge, two lawyers, and a client on trial for stealing. Have the lawyers present their sides and have the judge make a ruling. Have children write up the proceedings as a play.

Using informal and intimate language   Young learners must come to recognize and use language at different levels of formality in their writing if they are to become truly proficient. This range of formality-informality levels can be provided in activities such as these.

Have the students write jokes and riddles for sharing with the class.

Have the children role-play a familiar scene, such as a father or mother coming home from work or children playing together on a playground.

Have children write a scene for a play focusing on a family dinner table with a mother, father, grandmother, and two children present. Provide more details if necessary.

Have students write up accounts of oral interviews with family members.

PURPOSES IN WRITING

The varying purposes for writing are inextricably bound up in other concepts and skills of composition. However, the elementary teacher must plan over the course of the year to assure that all critical writing purposes are covered and, thus, accord the concept a special place in the writing curriculum. Ideas and activities modeled after the following can help assure this coverage and instruction.

Writing to Inform

Ask the students to write directions on how to construct something or how to play a game (this might be graphically portrayed earlier in show-and-tell).

Ask the students to write out directions on how to get to their house from the school for a new friend in town.

Have the students prepare a paper describing their favorite hike, food, or vacation.

Have the children relate to the class something that happened to them on the way to school or at home the previous evening.

Writing to Describe

Provide the students with a picture of an active scene and ask them to write a description of what is happening. (The type of composition can vary depending on the audience—whether oneself, a good friend, or a general or unknown audience.)

Ask the students to choose a friend in class. Have them write a description of the person (including references to clothing, personal appearance, and behavior). When finished, suggest that children read their descriptions and see if the rest of the class can guess the person being described.

Have the students describe a room at home. Remind them to use a logical order, for example, to go from left to right or from the center to the walls. Or, they might describe the walls first, then the windows and curtains, then the furniture, and other accessories.

Place three or four objects on your desk. Ask the students to choose one silently, then write a description of it. Have individual children read their descriptions and see whether the remainder of the class can guess which object is being described.

Writing to Inquire (ask)

Have students pretend they are going on a trip to their favorite city. They will be there for two days. Ask them to write a letter to the chamber of commerce inquiring about things they might do or places they might see.

Tell the students that a new friend in school who has just moved to town has asked them over to visit. Request that they write a series of questions they would ask to help them find their new friend's house.

Inform the students that a police officer will be visiting class soon (actually arrange it, if possible). Request that they write down a number of questions they would like to ask the officer.

Writing to Persuade (argue)

Ask children to take a position about how to spend a day—at the zoo, on a picnic, or playing with friends. Encourage them to use one of the argument forms considered earlier or the claim-support-conclusion model discussed in the first strand of the composition curriculum framework.

Pair students up and ask them to discuss with their peer how best to convince the rest of their class that they should take a trip to the zoo rather than to the local fire department (or vice versa). Have them jointly write their proposal for the rest of the class.

Ask some students to pretend that they are the judge in a trial. (Prepare a short scenario about a cookie thief in the cafeteria.) Ask others to be lawyers for the defense or the prosecution. Depending upon their assigned roles, ask each to write an argument or a judgment regarding the case.

Writing to Direct

Ask children to write a set of directions on how to assemble a new toy or how to play a game or how to get to a location in the community.

Have students pretend they are directors in a short play (provide a script if possible). Tell them to write a set of directions for the stage crew to use in preparing the set.

Have children pretend to be doctors who have patients who have broken legs. Ask them to write out directions to their patients on how to "take care" of their injury.

Writing to Enjoy

Consider the range of activities in the creative writing section of strand 1. In addition, the following activities should be considered.

Ask students to provide detailed descriptions for characters you invent, for example:

1. Weird Willy—an octopus in the Los Angeles Zoo.
2. Anxious Ann—an impatient little girl who does not get along with other people.
3. Silly Sam—a boy who would rather play jokes on people than eat.

Have students make up stories using some of the above characters in central roles.

Provide unusual photographs or art objects for children. Have them jot down individual words that describe how the object or photo makes them feel or reflects their interpretation of it. Ask them to use this information to write a short poem about the object or photo.

Ask the students to think of "weird" things to write about. List these on 5 × 8 note cards and file them. Tell the class the topics will be used later in writing assignments. Occasionally choose a card and talk about the subject's possible use with the class. What are some compositions that might be appropriate about it? What are some characters that might appear in a story about it?

SELECTED REFERENCES ON THE IMPINGING FACTORS OF CIRCUMSTANCE

Composition in the Language Arts, Grades 1–8: An Instructional Framework. Madison, Wis.: Wisconsin Department of Public Instruction, 1976.

A Curriculum for English: Poetry for the Elementary Grades. Lincoln, Neb.: University of Nebraska Press, 1966.

WIGGINTON, E.   *The Foxfire Book.* New York: Doubleday, 1972. (There are a number of succeeding numbered volumes in this series.)

Evaluating Writing and Monitoring Writing Progress

<table>
<tr><td>chapter
7</td></tr>
</table>

EVALUATING WRITING

There are two important purposes for evaluating the writing of students. One purpose is to gain an overall accurate picture of how effective the writing program in the school is. This information is important in determining matters such as curriculum development or modification, staff development, program design, and for general administrative and curriculum policy formulations.

However, the most important reason for writing evaluation is instructional. The teacher needs to know where writing progress has taken place and where assistance is needed. Further, it is important for the child to see growth—improvement in the writing produced. The student also needs to develop a positive attitude toward evaluation. All writers subject their efforts to public scrutiny at some time. Further, all of us write with limited vision. We often are so close to our writing that even errors or awkward constructions that are obvious to another escape our own observation. The writer should welcome critical comments and evaluation by others and, at the same time, become an objective self-critic to whatever extent possible.

It is easier to point out the importance of evaluation, however, than to address specifically *how* writing should be evaluated. The two most troublesome problems for the teacher who wishes to use writing evaluation to improve instruction are the great number of students (often 25 to 35 per class) and the timing of the evaluation.

With large numbers of papers to examine, close critical reading and marking can become a practical impossibility. Further, experts acknowledge that the point where the writer can best benefit from a critic is *during* the writing act and not after. Papers returned a day or two or even later after writing has taken place find the writer in a different time frame and in a different mental set. The most effective critiquing of writing from an instructional point of view is during the act—even if it means interrupting the process. It does appear that such approaches should be used selectively and not as a single evaluation method, however.

James Britton and others suggest that the writer writes in three substantially different "voices," the *expressive,* the *transactional,* and the *poetic.* The expressive voice is relatively private and free-flowing. It is used most often in such writing media as journals and personal letters. It is the voice of the writer first exploited successfully by the young child, who then moves to the other two voices. The transactional writing voice is utilized in much of our exposition and narration. Compositions intended to inform, describe, explain, and persuade usually are written in this voice. The poetic voice is reserved for aesthetic expression.

Writing in the expressive voice is most amenable to the interruption mode of evaluation. Transactional voice and poetic voice writing are more adaptable to "after-the-fact evaluation."

One particularly adaptable modification of the "getting-into-the-writing-act" kind of evaluation is use of a "dialogue journal." The student writes entries on the lefthand side of a page. The teacher skims the entries, and at appropriate spots, writes back to the student on the righthand side. Over time there evolves an ongoing journal dialogue perhaps similar to the following:

STUDENT ENTRIES	TEACHER RESPONSES
Well, I got my new coat today. I think I should have been happier but I wasn't.	
	You're kidding! A new coat and not happy! What's your problem?
I really wanted a long grey one but Mom wouldn't spring for it. I mean I don't ask for that much.	
	Was it that much more, or were there other reasons your mother balked?
Oh, I had just gotten some other new clothes and Christmas is coming up. You know, I'll bet that she's planning on . . .	

The above technique is only one part of a plan for writing evaluation, however. And an overall plan is critical if the program is to reflect writer growth and improvement. The following guidelines and suggestions should prove helpful in designing such a plan.

1. *Be consistent* It is important that students know what to expect when a teacher responds to their work. Children learning to write must establish an anticipatory attitude that is positive. Teachers who are not fair and consistent in their evaluations leave them confused and frustrated.

One critical principle that should be established is that some writing that children do should be largely immune to *any* evaluation. Perhaps poetic voice writing, that in the creative modes, should receive more of this "hands-off" treatment than any other. This is not to suggest that creative writing should not be evaluated, but rather that more of it should go unevaluated than other modes or should receive less specific commentary at times than other modes. Certainly, all modes of children's writing in all "voices" should be treated with varying degrees of commentary, evaluation, and instructional suggestions.

2. *Build variety into the evaluation plan*   Some writing should be evaluated "holistically," that is, with a general response to its overall quality. Comments on strengths and weaknesses are appropriate. Undue weight is not given to mechanics or form per se. Holistic evaluation enables the teacher to respond to a large number of papers without devoting substantial energy and time to detailed scoring or commentary. This method of evaluation also enables the teacher to maintain an informal assessment of the progress of the class as a whole. Remember, too, that placing individual student papers on an overhead projector for class scrutiny can be a delicate matter and should be done only after class rapport is established and there is a positive attitude about evaluation as a part of the writing process.

3. *Be comprehensive*   All basic skills and concepts central to quality writing must be evaluated. They do not all warrant equal attention, and the order of their consideration is not tightly fixed as far as writing development is concerned. This is an area where curriculum articulation through the grades is important. There must be a scope and sequence of skills and concepts with enough specificity elaborated at each grade level for the teacher to have guidelines for the development of a specific writing evaluation plan.

Certainly at every grade some evaluation must be made of:

1. *The student's comfort and facility with the writing process.* Does the student effectively build from prewriting to writing to follow-up, including but not restricted to revision? Is fluency adequate, comfortable, and often self-generated by the student? Does the student *enjoy* discussing his or her writing and the writing of others with peers?

2. *The student's mastery of critical structures and forms central to writing.* Does the student reflect enough concern for the public appearance potential of his or her writing? Are punctuation, capitalization, and spelling matters of personal pride in a completed written piece? Has the student developed a reasonable syntactic repertoire from which to draw in the writing? Is the sentence structure not only grammatically acceptable but also stylistically appropriate? Is paragraphing tight and logically linked? Does the student show a developing sense of the relationships among the forms or modes of writing chosen (narrative, expository, creative) and the various elements, concepts, and structures appropriate to each mode?

3. *The student's mastery of the organizational elements critical to effective composition.* Is logic reasonably reflected? Do conclusions follow from premises stated or positions taken? Are transitional devices and expressions used where and when necessary? Is topic sentence and thesis assertion use acceptable?

4. *The student's presentation of ideas and content.* Is it developmentally appropriate? Does it show acceptable maturity and depth, and reflect a desire to be imaginative and interesting? Are topics chosen which show perception of audience and purpose? Are facts and concepts presented that develop a thesis or main idea? Does the student know when more information is needed or when too much has been given?

Although not an exhaustive list, questions such as these should be integral to any writing evaluation plan developed by the elementary and middle school teacher.

A second type of evaluation is called "focused feedback" evaluation. In this system the teacher highlights a specific writing skill or concept that will be critiqued in a given writing assignment. For example, the focus for Andy Jones in this particular assignment will be upon spelling. Other skills and concepts in his writing assignment will receive only passing attention or comment. In a later assignment the focus might be upon an appropriate topic sentence or organization or sentence structure (perhaps whatever needs greatest remediation). Focused feedback allows the teacher to individualize writing instruction to some extent by focusing upon the most serious writing development problems of different children.

It must be remembered, however, that the writing skills and concepts to be evaluated are not to be selected arbitrarily. A checklist of key skills and concepts derived from the composition curriculum framework or similarly comprehensive schema should be used for planning and monitoring progress.

A third important type of writing evaluation is peer evaluation. Students read and critique each other's writing and then conference over the papers. The easiest form of peer review from a classroom management standpoint is to do it by pairs. After this has been done long enough for students to be comfortable with the process, peer review can be done in small groups (four to five students per group).

A modification of this process for whole class involvement is to use the overhead projector, examining individual papers that have been made into transparencies (opaque projectors, of course, are excellent, since actual papers can be used; however, opaque projectors are no longer commonly found in schools).

MONITORING WRITING GROWTH

Evaluating student writing and monitoring the student's writing development are part and parcel of the same thing. Many of the ideas presented in the first section of this chapter, for example, clearly presume that student profiles and records are being maintained. But a monitoring system has a valuable role that goes beyond evaluation per se. A well-designed monitoring system enables the teacher to individualize writing instruction in an effective way. It provides longitudinal information on each child in enough detail to allow pinpointing instructional needs.

Although there is a wide variety of possible means of monitoring writing development, there are certain features they all have in common.

1. There is a planned ongoing record-keeping system. Individual student file folders are maintained with representative samples of student writing included.

2. There is a checklist of skills, concepts, and processes of writing with a scoring system that is utilized to identify individuals' particular areas of growth and need. This checklist should derive from a comprehensive framework for a well-articulated and well-sequenced composition program.

3. There is some type of diagnostic system structured into the monitoring system. Usually, this includes brief objective tests that attempt to pinpoint mechanical, structural, and usage types of basic errors. In addition, there are more descriptive normative types of diagnosis applied to samples of student writing. The latter often include measures of students' syntactic fluency by use of technical measures such as T-unit scoring and some assessment of stylistic choices for their appropriateness in a given writing task.

4. Time is scheduled for individual student conferences to discuss writing projects and practices. These conferences are built into daily operations of the classroom so that the student comes to see them as a normal and expected part of the instructional program.

5. There are planned conferences of the teaching staff to share information about student growth. And a system exists for moving forward through the grades the student writing folders, including recommendations for efforts by the teacher at the next grade level.

6. There is an overall school plan for assessing writing achievement and an ongoing dialogue about the nature and function of a composition curriculum.

Various approaches to monitoring in the composition program include additional features. The above, however, represent the most fundamental.

Perhaps the most important characteristic of a high-quality writing curriculum is that teachers and students and parents talk about the writing program. For them, writing represents a fundamental part of their daily lives and is most likely assumed to be central to their literacy. One can ask for little more than that about this critical part of our education.

SELECTED REFERENCES
ON WRITING EVALUATION
AND PROGRAM MONITORING

COOPER, R., and ODELL, L. *Evaluating Writing.* Urbana, Ill.: National Council of Teachers of English, 1977.

DIEDERICH, P. *Measuring Growth in English.* Urbana, Ill.: National Council of Teachers of English, 1974.

FAGAN, W.; COOPER, C.; and JENSEN, J. *Measures for Research and Evaluation in the English Language Arts.* Urbana, Ill.: National Council of Teachers of English, 1975.

SPANDEL, V. *Classroom Applications of Writing Assessment: A Teacher's Handbook.* Portland, Oreg.: Northwest Regional Educational Laboratory, 1981.

SPANDEL, V., and STIGGINS, R. J. *Direct Measures of Writing Skill: Issues and Applications.* Portland, Oreg.: Northwest Regional Educational Laboratory, 1981.
Handbook for Planning an Effective Writing Program. Sacramento: California State Department of Education, 1982.

SELECTED BIBLIOGRAPHY

BEARDSLEY, M. *Writing with Reason.* Englewood Cliffs, N.J.: Prentice-Hall, Inc., 1976.

BRANDT, W., and OTHERS. *The Craft of Writing.* Englewood Cliffs, N.J.: Prentice-Hall, Inc., 1969.

BRITTON, J., and OTHERS. *The Development of Writing Abilities (11–18).* London: Macmillan Education Ltd., 1975.

COODY, B., and NELSON, DAVID. *Teaching Elementary Language Arts: A Literature Approach.* Belmont, Calif.: Wadsworth Publishing Co., 1982.

COOPER, C., and ODELL, L., eds. *Research on Composing: Points of Departure.* Urbana, Ill.: National Council of Teachers of English, 1978.

CRAMER, R. *Children's Writing and Language Growth.* Columbus, Ohio: Charles E. Merrill, 1978.

FADIMAN, C., and HOWARD, J. *Empty Pages: A Search for Writing Competence in School and Society.* Belmont, Calif.: Fearon Pitman Publishers, 1979.

GRIFFIN, C. W., ed. *Teaching Writing in All Disciplines.* San Francisco: Jossey-Bass, 1982.

HALEY-JAMES, S., ed. *Perspectives on Writing in Grades 1–8.* Urbana, Ill.: National Council of Teachers of English, 1981.

Individualized Language Arts. Weehawken, N.J.: Weehawken Board of Education, 1974.

KRESS, G. *Learning to Write.* London: Routledge and Kegan Paul, 1982.

KROLL, B., and R. VANN, eds. *Exploring Speaking-Writing Relationships: Connections and Contrasts.* Urbana, Ill.: National Council of Teachers of English, 1981.

PIERSON, H. *Teaching Writing.* Englewood Cliffs, N.J.: Prentice-Hall, 1972.

SHUMAN, R. B., ed. *Education in the 80's: English.* Washington, D.C.: National Education Association, 1981.

STEWIG, JOHN. *Teaching Language Arts in Early Childhood.* New York: CBS College Publishing, 1982.

TEMPLE, C., and others. *The Beginnings of Writings.* Boston: Allyn and Bacon, 1982.

TIEDT, I. M., and others. *Teaching Writing in K–8 Classrooms: The Time Has Come.* Englewood Cliffs, N.J.: Prentice-Hall, 1983.

WALSHE, R. D., ed. *Donald Graves in Australia—"Children Want to Write . . ."* Exeter, N.H.: Heinemann Educational Books, 1982.

WIENER, H. S. *The Writing Room.* New York: Oxford University Press, 1981.

WOOD, BARBARA S. *Children and Communication: Verbal and Nonverbal Language.* Englewood Cliffs, N.J.: Prentice-Hall, 1981.

Index